The Beginner's Book of Erotic Wizardry

Mastering the Mystical Aspects of Love and Desire

Christopher Wright

Table of Contents

INTRODUCTION

"The Beginner's Book of Erotic Wizardry: Mastering the Mystical Aspects of Love and Desire" takes readers on a seductive trip into the world of mystical pleasure as it explores the fascinating confluence of magic and sensuality. This book, written by famed wizardry practitioner and intimacy specialist Christopher Wright, reveals the dark secrets of using magical energies to improve and intensify one's feelings of love and desire.

"The Beginner's Book of Erotic Wizardry" is essentially a thorough manual for anyone interested in delving into the deep relationships that exist between sensuality and spirituality. Wright expertly combines conventional knowledge with cutting-edge understanding to offer readers doable methods and ceremonies that help them rediscover the ethereal elements of their romantic relationships.

The book exposes readers to a wide range of magical techniques, including astral projection, tantric rituals, divination, and spellcasting. Readers are invited to go on a transforming voyage of self-discovery and sensuous exploration as each chapter unfolds like a captivating incantation.

Drawing on a wide range of mystical traditions and esoteric teachings, Wright provides readers with an all-encompassing perspective on eroticism, stressing the significance of intentionality, mindfulness, and permission in developing satisfying and empowering close connections.

Inviting readers to embrace their intrinsic magical potential and discover the secret depths of their sensual identities, "The Beginner's Book of Erotic Wizardry" exceeds the bounds of conventional self-help literature with its beautiful prose and vibrant images. This book claims to arouse the latent powers of enchantment that are dormant inside every one of us, regardless of our level of experience. It is a great way to start a new practice or broaden your skill set. people travel entirely. Additionally, in the field of education, adaptive learning platforms are helping students reach their full potential by customizing their learning experiences to meet their unique needs.

However, these developments also bring significant societal ramifications and moral problems. Embracing the machine learning revolution will present obstacles such as the possible exacerbation of social inequality, worries about data privacy and security, bias in algorithmic decision-making, and the loss of jobs to automation.

We encourage readers to investigate the advantages and disadvantages of this revolutionary technology as we set out on this voyage into the realm of algorithms. Our objective is to enable people, institutions, and decision-makers to effectively traverse the intricacies of our progressively algorithmic society by cultivating a sophisticated comprehension of machine learning and its consequences.

CHAPTER I

Understanding the Mystical Energies of Desire

Exploring the connection between magic and desire

Magic is a mysterious energy that has fascinated people for ages and has a close relationship with the complex web of human desires. The allure of magic entwined with our deepest desires shaped beliefs, communities, and even personal aspirations, from ancient civilizations to contemporary ones. This article explores historical, cultural, and psychological aspects as it sets out to disentangle the complex relationship between magic and desire.

The ability to create the seemingly impossible and to go beyond the limits of the natural world is at the core of magic. Societies all across the world have used magic in various forms throughout history because they believed it could change the course of events and grant wishes. Magicians tried to use rituals, spells, or incantations to control supernatural energies in order to fulfill their desires for power, riches, or love. Magic's attraction stems from its ability to grant control over destiny, fulfilling wishes that appear unattainable through traditional methods.

The yearning for love and closeness is one of the core needs that motivates the study of magic. Magic is frequently used in literature and mythology to set romantic relationships in motion, helping lovers overcome challenges and come together in the face of overwhelming difficulties. Invoking the mystical to create connections that go beyond the ordinary, spells and potions are designed to arouse feelings of desire and attraction. Magic becomes a powerful instrument of manipulation in the world of desire, obscuring the distinction between genuine affection and manufactured charm.

Additionally, the need for control and mastery over oneself and the outside world connects with magic. The archetype of the witch or sorcerer represents the desire to control natural forces and rise above human limitations. Practitioners attempt to manipulate reality to their will by using rituals and esoteric knowledge to gain power that is beyond the reach of ordinary people. Such power is alluring not just because it can fulfill personal needs but also because it has the capacity to influence historical events. But as stories of hubris and fallout illustrate, the cost of using magic to gain power is frequently high and serves as a warning against unbridled ambition.

Magic reflects society's ideals and objectives in addition to personal wishes. Magical practices provide a way to communicate with supernatural forces and ask for direction when needed. They are often intricately entwined with religious beliefs and rituals in many cultures. Magic offers a means for people to seek answers to existential issues and negotiate life's difficulties, from ancient oracles to contemporary divination. In addition, magic frequently functions as a vehicle for cultural expression, upholding customs and ideas that have been handed down through the ages and influencing societal identities and worldviews.

The relationship between magic and desire is not without its complications and paradoxes, though. Although magic involves inherent risks and uncertainties, it also holds the potential of fulfillment. Because wants are inherently complex and subject to change, pursuing them by supernatural methods may have unexpected results. Furthermore, the moral ramifications of using magic to alter reality pose concerns about the nature of moral responsibility and free choice. The price of achieving one's objectives is sometimes represented in stories of Faustian bargains and dealings with the devil as the forfeiture of one's soul, serving as a sobering reminder of the ethical quandaries that arise while pursuing power.

Psychology's investigation of human motivation and cognition finds echoes in the relationship between magic and desire. Psychologists believe that human conduct is fundamentally shaped by desires, which influence our feelings, thoughts, and behaviors. Conversely, magic functions at the level of belief and imagination, reaching into the mind's subconscious to arouse emotions of amazement, suspense, and wonder. From a psychological perspective, magic's appeal stems from its capacity to inspire awe and suspend disbelief, providing a psychological escape from the constraints of mundane existence.

Moreover, the study of desire and magic illuminates the function of metaphor and symbolism in human awareness. Deeply symbolic and ritualistic practices are found in many magical traditions; they act as a conduit between the conscious and unconscious minds. By externalizing and giving expression to impulses through symbolism, people are able to face and work with their deepest desires. Magical symbols, which encode desires into tangible forms that can be manipulated and modified, have been used as vehicles for personal and collective aspirations for centuries, from ancient talismans to contemporary sigils.

In summary, the relationship between magic and desire is a complex and multidimensional phenomenon that cuts beyond psychological, historical, and cultural barriers. Magic continues to captivate the human imagination, from ancient rituals to modern activities, providing a window into the depths of the human psyche and the mysteries of the cosmos. Fundamentally, magic is the never-ending pursuit of manifesting the extraordinary and beyond the bounds of the ordinary; it is the echo of the age-old human longing to find fulfillment in the mysterious domains of the supernatural.

Introduction to different mystical energies and their influence on love

Across cultures and historical periods, mystical energies and spiritual beliefs have been deeply entwined with love, the most fundamental human emotion. The goal of this section is to offer an essential examination of the many mystical energies and how love is affected by them. The fields of mysticism offer a wide range of viewpoints on the nature of love and its relationship to higher powers, from traditional wisdom to modern activities.

In Eastern spiritual traditions, the heart chakra is one of the most well-known mystical energies connected to love. The heart chakra, also called Anahata, is said to be the source of love, compassion, and emotional equilibrium in Buddhist and Hindu beliefs. It's said that people who have an open and aligned energy center form strong bonds with others, which promote harmonious relationships and unconditional love. Practices that open the heart chakra and allow unconditional love to flow, such as yoga, meditation, and also energy healing, can help to balance and activate the heart chakra.

Beyond romantic and interpersonal interactions, the idea of love is frequently examined in Western esoteric traditions through the prism of divine or spiritual love. Religious traditions like Kabbalah and Christian mysticism, which emphasize the transformative power of divine love as the ultimate source of satisfaction and harmony, are known for their mystic teachings. By engaging in activities like prayer, meditation, and mystical devotion, adherents aim to develop a closer relationship with God and let love seep into all facets of their lives and interpersonal interactions.

In addition, a number of metaphysical and energy healing modalities employ crystals, herbs, and other natural materials to increase attraction and love. In the field of crystal therapy, love, and relationships are frequently connected to gemstones like rose quartz, which are thought to emit energies of empathy, compassion, and emotional healing. Comparably, for ages, rituals, and spells to draw love, promote closeness, and settle disputes in partnerships have included herbs and plants. Through the use of nature's subtle energies, these techniques produce resonance and alignment with the vibrations of love.

In addition, the age-old discipline of astrology provides an understanding of the ethereal forces involved in romantic and interpersonal interactions. Astrology sees the universe as a dynamic system of planetary forces interacting to shape human experience and behavior. Astrologers aim to identify the underlying patterns and potentials in relationships by analyzing birth charts and planetary alignments to unveil the hidden dynamics of love and compatibility. People are better equipped to handle the complexity of love by being aware of the cosmic elements at play.

Modern metaphysical practices like the Law of Attraction and energy manifestation have been more popular in recent years due to their emphasis on conscious creation and deliberate living, in addition to these traditional mystical energies. According to the Law of Attraction, people may create their desires—including love and relationships—by focusing their intentions and thinking positively. It is said that like attracts like. Aiming to attract compatible mates and foster meaningful relationships, practitioners match their thoughts, emotions, and actions with the vibration of love.

But it's crucial to proceed cautiously and with discernment while investigating mystical forces and how they affect love. These techniques cannot replace real connection, communication, and respect between partners in a relationship, even though they can provide insightful advice and encouragement on the path to love. Love is a complex feeling with emotional, psychological, and spiritual aspects. As such, its fundamental nature cannot be boiled down to a set of metaphysical practices or rituals.

To sum up, investigating mystical energies and how they affect love can lead to a greater comprehension and appreciation of the intricacies of interpersonal relationships. Mysticism offers a wide range of viewpoints on the nature of love and its relationship to higher powers, whether through traditional wisdom or modern practices.

Exercises to attune oneself to these energies

Developing a healthy relationship with the world, expanding one's awareness, and making connections with subtle forces are all necessary steps in attuning oneself to mystical energies. Using lessons from modern metaphysics, holistic therapeutic techniques, and ancient wisdom traditions, this section examines a variety of exercises and practices meant to promote this attunement. Through these practices, people can become more attuned to mystical energies and more in tune with cosmic awareness.

A fundamental technique for connecting with mystical forces, meditation provides a road to inner peace, clarity, and heightened awareness. People can attune to the subtle vibrations of the cosmos, open their hearts, and quiet their minds through meditation. The relationship with mystical powers can be strengthened and a sense of unity with the cosmos can be developed through techniques like as visualization, loving-kindness meditation, and mindfulness meditation. People who regularly practice meditation can develop their intuitive abilities and become attuned to the ever-present streams of divine energy.

Energy healing techniques like Reiki, Qi Gong, and Pranic Healing are effective means of connecting to mystical energies and reestablishing equilibrium in the body, mind, and spirit, in addition to meditation. These techniques facilitate the free flow of life force energy, eliminate blockages, and release stagnant energy by interacting with the body's subtle energy systems. People can attune to the healing energies of the universe and become channels for divine love and light by participating in energy healing sessions or learning how to channel energy on their own. They can become attuned to subtle energy cues and gain an understanding of the interdependence of all things with consistent practice.

In addition, spending time in nature is a powerful way to reestablish a connection with the Earth's inherent rhythms and tune into mystical energies. The soul is grounded, renewed, and inspired by nature, which also provides a haven for spiritual regeneration and heavenly communication. People can learn to connect with the elemental energies of the Earth, air, fire, water, and spirit by engaging in practices like elemental rites, nature meditation, and forest bathing. People can establish a strong sense of connectivity with all life and align with the fundamental energies of creation by fully immersing themselves in the beauty and majesty of the natural world.

Furthermore, working with sacred symbols, archetypes, and rituals can be a powerful way to open up to mystical energies and reach higher awareness levels. Symbols of significant spiritual meaning, like the Tree of Life, the Sri

Yantra, and the Flower of Life, are thought to contain cosmic wisdom and universal truths. People can attune to the archetypal energies these symbols represent and awaken dormant portions of their own consciousness by meditating on them, calling upon their power, and incorporating them into rituals and ceremonies. Invoking divine presence and tuning into mystical energies can also be facilitated by rituals like sacred ceremonies, blessings, and consecrations.

In addition, sound healing provides a transforming way to balance the body's and soul's subtle vibrations and attune oneself to mystical energies. Sound possesses the ability to resonate with our innermost being, bringing dormant potentials to life and promoting holistic healing. Attuning to the cosmic symphony of creation, releasing energetic blockages, and accessing altered levels of consciousness are all possible using methods like drumming, singing bowls, toning, and chanting. People can attune to the vibrational frequencies of love, harmony, and oneness by using music as a tool for self-expression, change, and spiritual communication.

In summary, the process of becoming attuned to mystical energies is a profound and transforming one that calls for commitment, purpose, and an open mind to the secrets of the cosmos. By engaging in techniques like energy healing, sound healing, nature immersion, ritual, meditation, and sacred symbols, people can become more in tune with the universal consciousness and strengthen their connection to the divine. People can become more aware of their actual nature as spiritual beings and live lives that are characterized by wisdom, love, and compassion by tuning into these mystical energies.

CHAPTER II

The Art of Sensual Spellcasting

Harnessing the power of intention and visualization in love and desire

Throughout history, people from all cultures have acknowledged the power of intention and visualization as practical means of bringing dreams to life and influencing events. These methods take on a deeper meaning when they are applied to the domain of love and desire. They provide a means of drawing in meaningful connections, fostering satisfying relationships, and living as the purest forms of love. This section draws on scientific data, contemporary metaphysical teachings, and ancient wisdom traditions to examine the concepts and methods of using intention and imagery in matters of love.

Fundamentally, the intention is the deliberate focus of one's thoughts, feelings, and energies on a particular result or objective. When it comes to love and desire, intention acts as a catalyst, bringing people into harmony with the vibration of love and giving them the ability to draw in and nurture deep connections. People are able to construct a potent, energetic blueprint that attracts riches and love into their lives by establishing specific goals that are grounded in authenticity, clarity, and genuine desire. The intention is what propels people to materialize in the field of love, be they for a romantic connection, to strengthen current relationships, or to embody self-acceptance and love.

The process of forming vivid mental images or situations that reflect one's intended results is known as visualization, on the other side. People can program their subconscious minds to coincide with their intentions by immersing themselves in the experience of love and desire through the use of their imagination and senses. Through the use of visualization techniques like mental rehearsal, vision planning, and guided imagery, people can create realistic images of themselves experiencing all forms of love, from passionate romanticism to pure compassion. By means of regular application, visualization modifies brain connections, fosters an optimistic outlook, and strengthens the attraction of purpose, thus opening doors to the achievement of intended results.

The transformational power of purpose and visualization in matters of love and desire has long been acknowledged by ancient wisdom traditions like yoga, meditation, and Tantra. In the yoga tradition, practitioners use the power of Sankalpa, or sacred intention, to bring their innermost wishes into reality and connect with their ultimate purpose. By using techniques like yoga nidra and pranayama, people achieve a profound level of relaxation and openness, which permits their intentions to infiltrate the subconscious and establish themselves in the rich soil of the soul. Tantric traditions similarly place great emphasis on developing bhava, or heavenly sensation, as a way to tune into the ecstasy of love that permeates the universe. By combining intention with emotion, imagination with embodiment, and spiritual enlightenment with union with the divine, Tantra offers a comprehensive approach to harnessing the power of love and desire.

Modern metaphysical beliefs also provide valuable frameworks for using intention and imagery in the pursuit of love and desire, such as the Law of Attraction and energy manifestation. According to the Law of Attraction, people can intentionally attract the experiences they want by directing their thoughts, feelings, and behaviors toward the vibrational frequency of love. This principle states that like attracts like. People can rewire their subconscious minds and strengthen the magnetic pull of their intentions by engaging in techniques like scripting, gratitude journaling, and affirmations. This will help them attract abundance and love into their lives. Comparably, energy manifestation methods like Reality Transurfing and Quantum Jumping provide sophisticated instruments for negotiating alternative universes and intentionally directing the course of one's life experiences. People can quantum leap into their preferred reality and embody the love and joy they seek by mastering the power of intention and vision.

Moreover, studies in science have started to illuminate the effectiveness of intention and imagery in fostering favorable results in the domain of love and desire. Research in the domains of neuroscience, psychoneuroimmunology, and quantum physics has uncovered the significant influence of concentrated attention and mental imagery on mental and emotional states, as well as physical health. According to neuroimaging research, the act of envisioning good outcomes triggers the same brain circuits as experiencing them, resulting in alterations in behavior, physiology, and perception. Furthermore, studies on the placebo effect have shown how belief and expectation can affect subjective experiences and therapeutic processes. People can use the mind-body-spirit system's intrinsic ability to generate the conditions necessary for love and fulfillment by using intention and imagery.

Finally, the ability to materialize love and desire in all of its manifestations can be achieved through the transformative power of intention and imagery. The concepts and techniques of intention and visualization, whether derived from scientific studies, contemporary metaphysical teachings, or old wisdom traditions, offer a valuable framework for harmonizing with the vibration of love and co-creating a reality based on genuineness, joy, and connection. People can realize their full creative potential, overcome obstacles, and embody the purest forms of love in their relationships and daily lives by using intention and visualization.

Crafting and casting spells for enhancing sensuality

The study of human impulses, such as the amplification of sensuality and the strengthening of close relationships, has always been entwined with the craft of creating and using spells. Spells, with their roots in archaic customs and rich symbolism, provide a way to focus intention, energy, and ceremonial action in order to bring about desired results. Spells are potent instruments for stimulating the senses, developing erotic energy, and creating a stronger bond with oneself and others when they are used in the context of sensuality. The concepts, methods, and moral issues surrounding the creation and use of spells to increase sensuality are explored in this section, which draws from a variety of mystical traditions, modern occult practices, and approaches to sexual empowerment.

In spellcraft, the notion of intention—the deliberate focus of one's energy, emotions, and desires toward a particular sensuous result—lays the foundation for increasing sensuality. Practitioners must be clear about their intentions and make sure they are in line with their highest good and innermost aspirations before beginning any spellwork. A clear and focused goal forms the basis of any spell that aims to deepen intimacy, awaken desire, or boost pleasure. Through the potent alchemy of magic, practitioners create the conditions for the realization of their sensual wants by clearly and firmly stating their goals.

A crucial part of spellcraft for increasing sensuality is visualization, which enables practitioners to fully conceive and embody the sexual feelings they wish to have. The sensations, feelings, and situations connected to enhanced sensuality are brought to life for practitioners through guided imagery, sensory visualization, and creative visualization approaches. Practitioners link their thoughts and energies with the vibrational frequency of sensuality by activating the subconscious mind via the use of intention and imagination. When practitioners visualize themselves feeling fulfilled, connected, and pleasurable during their sensory experiences, it acts as a catalyst to bring desire into reality.

Furthermore, as symbols are potent means of directing energy, intention, and meaning, their use is essential in spellcraft to increase sensuality. Symbols are loaded with archetypal power and global meaning, signifying elemental energies and primeval forces, and can range from ancient talismans to contemporary sigils. Symbols like hearts, roses, and mirrors can be used by practitioners to conjure feelings of passion, love, and introspection when creating spells for sexuality. Through the incorporation of symbolic resonance into their spells, practitioners strengthen the intent behind them and create a symbolic bridge connecting the spiritual and material worlds.

In spellcraft for sensuality enhancement, ritualistic action is the material manifestation of intention and visualization; practitioners perform symbolic gestures, movements, and ceremonies to bring about the intended results. Rituals create a concentrated, energetic environment where magic can happen by acting as receptacles for sacred time and space. As they engage in communal ceremonies or solo rituals, practitioners bring intention, mindfulness, and reverence to everything they do. Lighting candles, making incense, calling upon deities, or chanting incantations are a few examples of rituals that can be performed to heighten the spell's energetic charge and synchronize the performer with the flow of sensual energy.

When using spellcraft to increase sensuality, practitioners must approach their job with integrity, respect, and permission. As such, ethical issues are crucial. Spells should never be used to oppress or control others; instead, they should be used to provide people the freedom to explore and express their own desires freely. In addition, practitioners need to consider the possible repercussions of their choices and make sure that the ethical tenets of respect for one another and non-harm constitute the foundation of their spells. In terms of sensuality, consent is crucial, and practitioners should always get everyone's permission before doing any spells that can influence the other person's sensory sensations.

To sum up, creating and using spells to heighten sensuality is an effective way to stimulate the senses, develop erotic energy, and strengthen close relationships. Spellcraft for sensuality is a transformative art that uses intention, vision, symbolism, and ritual to create desired outcomes in the domain of desire. Practitioners can access the sacred currents of sensuality and embrace the entirety of their sensual selves in all of their beauty, pleasure, and ecstasy by approaching their practice with mindfulness, integrity, and ethical awareness.

Practical exercise's for readers to try at home

Starting a path of self-discovery and personal development frequently entails doing hands-on activities that help people gain new insights, hone their abilities, and increase inner awareness. This section offers readers a range of doable activities in the areas of self-care, self-reflection, creativity, and mindfulness that they might attempt at home. Whether the goal is to improve mental health, stimulate creativity, or increase self-awareness, these activities provide practical and efficient means of supporting personal development and building a more contented existence.

The core techniques for developing present-moment awareness, lowering stress levels, and promoting inner calm are mindfulness exercises. A technique that helps with this is mindful breathing, when people concentrate on how their breath feels coming in and going out of their bodies. People can develop a sense of peace and centeredness in the middle of daily chaos by training their attention to the rhythm and flow of their breath, which serves as an anchor. Body scanning is another mindfulness technique where people deliberately examine their entire body, from head to toe, focusing on any tensions, sensations, or sore spots. Through the practice of attentive awareness of the body, people can reduce tension, encourage relaxation, and strengthen their bond with themselves.

Through self-expression, exploration, and discovery, creative exercises enable people to unlock their artistic potential and connect with their inner creativity. One such practice is freewriting, in which participants set a timer and write nonstop for that predetermined amount of time without pausing or self-censoring. By letting go of the inner critic and letting ideas and thoughts flow freely onto paper, people can reach more profound levels of insight and creativity. Collage-making is another creative activity where people collect words, pictures, and other objects that speak to them and arrange them on a canvas or piece of paper. People can access their subconscious minds, investigate themes and ideas, and produce a visual depiction of their inner world through this intuitive and enjoyable process.

Self-reflection exercises provide chances for introspection, understanding, and personal development, enabling people to get a deeper comprehension of who they are and the experiences they have had in life. Journaling is one such activity where people write openly and uncensored about their feelings, ideas, and experiences. By keeping a daily journal, people can discover patterns and themes, trace their own development over time, and obtain clarity, insight, and perspective on their deepest feelings and thoughts. A different kind of self-reflection is the thankfulness practice, where people routinely consider and express their gratitude for the wealth and blessings in their lives. This helps people develop an attitude of gratitude. People can change their perspective, create feelings of joy and happiness, and establish a stronger sense of connection with both themselves and the outside world by concentrating on the good parts of their experiences.

Exercises for self-care provide chances to nourish and care for the body, mind, and spirit, enabling people to put their health first and create harmony and balance in their lives. A mindful eating practice involves approaching meals with presence, awareness, and thankfulness, savoring each bite, and focusing on the sensory aspects of the meal. People can improve their digestion, enjoy meals more, and feel more connected to their bodies by developing a thoughtful relationship with food. Self-massage is an additional self-care practice where people knead, stroke, and apply pressure to various body parts using their hands or massage implements. People can reduce stress, encourage relaxation, and cultivate compassion and self-love by partaking in this loving and healing exercise.

To sum up, the practical tasks provide readers with valuable tools to experiment with, investigate, and incorporate into their everyday lives. Whether practicing self-care, self-reflection, mindfulness, or creativity, these activities offer chances for empowerment, personal development, and transformation. Readers can develop increased awareness, creativity, resilience, and well-being, as well as start a path of self-discovery and fulfillment by implementing these techniques into their daily lives.

CHAPTER III

Unlocking the Secrets of Erotic Alchemy

Delving into the concept of erotic alchemy and its transformative potential

Through the integration of erotic energy, erotic alchemy—a mystical and esoteric notion with roots in ancient wisdom traditions—holds the possibility of profound transformation and spiritual progress. This paper investigates the complex nature of erotic alchemy by following its principles, historical roots, and transformational potential in many metaphysical, cultural, and historical contexts. People can awaken to their full potential, solve the secrets of desire, and become the alchemical union of body, mind, and spirit by exploring the depths of erotic alchemy.

Fundamentally, the practice of transmuting basic or primal energy into refined and higher states of consciousness is the foundation of erotic alchemy. Inspired by the alchemical symbolism of turning lead into gold, sexual alchemy uses the raw strength of romantic energy to activate internal alchemical processes. Practitioners of erotic alchemy aim to enhance their sexual energies to higher vibrational levels by purifying, refining, and working with the elemental forces of ecstasy, desire, and arousal. By doing this, individuals discover the transformational power that lies within their sensory experiences and awakens to the sacred nature of sexuality.

The roots of erotic alchemy can be found in esoteric practices, mystery schools, and sacred texts from antiquity that praised sensual energy as a powerful tool for enlightenment and spiritual awakening. For instance, adherents of Tantric traditions perform ceremonies, exercises, and meditations with the aim of combining their inner masculine and feminine selves and harnessing the transforming potential of sexual energy. Analogously, in Taoist alchemy, practitioners nurture and energize their internal alchemical furnace by cultivating and circulating chi, or life force energy, throughout their bodies. The idea of erotic alchemy has been held in high regard as a sacred and transforming route to divine union throughout history and across all civilizations.

The development of sexual consciousness, or heightened awareness and sensitivity to the subtle forces of desire and arousal, is essential to the practice of erotic alchemy. For those who practice erotic alchemy, eroticism is not only physical or carnal; instead, it is a gateway to higher levels of consciousness, ecstatic connection, and spiritual communion. Practitioners can access the vast knowledge and healing potential of sexual energy by practicing presence, mindfulness, and intention in their erotic experiences. This allows them to transcend ego constraints and embrace the richness of their erotic identities.

In addition, the idea of erotic alchemy includes the alchemical mingling of masculine and feminine energy within the person, as well as the fusion of opposites and polarities. The union of the feminine Moon with the masculine Sun in alchemical symbolism signifies the emergence of wholeness and balance as well as the merging of opposing energies. Similar to this, those who practice erotic alchemy want to embrace the whole range of their erotic expression while balancing and harmonizing their masculine and feminine sides. Practitioners can embody the alchemical marriage of opposites within themselves and unleash the transforming potential of erotic energy by respecting and integrating both the light and shadow sides of their sexuality.

For those who have endured trauma, shame, or repression related to their sexuality, erotic alchemy provides a means of healing, emancipation, and empowerment. People can overcome personal constraints, cultural taboos, and societal conditioning that prevent them from freely expressing their sexuality by reclaiming and redefining their erotic identities. People can heal old wounds, dissolve energetic blockages, and develop a more loving and also harmonious relationship with their bodies and sexuality by engaging in techniques like conscious touch, erotic embodiment, and sexual healing. Through embracing one's erotic nature as a source of vigor, creativity, and strength, erotic alchemy facilitates personal development, self-discovery, and empowerment.

In summary, by integrating erotic energy, the idea of erotic alchemy provides a transforming road to awakening, healing, and self-realization. Erotic alchemy, which has its roots in age-old wisdom traditions, encourages people to investigate the holy secrets of ecstasy, arousal, and desire as doors to altered states of consciousness and spiritual connectedness. Practitioners of erotic alchemy can unlock the latent potential in their sensual experiences and set out on a path of profound transformation and self-discovery by adopting the concepts of transmutation, integration, and unity.

Techniques for transmuting sexual energy into spiritual growth

Frequently depicted as an innate power pulsating through our existence, sexual energy possesses the capacity to initiate significant metamorphosis and spiritual advancement. Many methods have been investigated throughout history and civilizations to harness and transform this powerful energy from something that is only for bodily pleasure into an instrument for spiritual awakening. People travel into the depths of their libido and discover the holy essence within the world of erotic wizardry. Here, we dive deeply into an in-depth examination of methods for transforming sexual energy into spiritual development, providing practices and insights for those just starting out on their path in the mysterious world of erotic sorcery. Transmuting sexual energy into spiritual progress begins with mindfulness. We can start to comprehend the finer points of our own sexual energy by developing awareness of our feelings, ideas, and physical experiences during intimate moments. By engaging in mindfulness exercises like breathwork, meditation, and sensory awareness, people can learn to notice their sexual sensations without getting overwhelmed by them.

This expanded consciousness enables the sexual energy to be redirected toward spiritual realization and higher realms of consciousness rather than just bodily fulfilment.

A technique to elevate the act of making love into a sacred and life-changing experience is through holy sexuality. Holy sexuality, which has its roots in old customs and spiritual teachings, highlights the close relationship between spirituality and sexuality.

Practitioners consider every moment as a chance for spiritual growth and communion, and they approach sexual encounters with attention, intention, and reverence. People can strengthen their bonds with the divine, their spouses, and themselves by creating holy spaces, having honest conversations, and bringing love and spiritual energy into the experience. Tantra is a rich tapestry of techniques and teachings for utilizing sexual energy for spiritual advancement, originating from ancient Indian traditions. The fundamental idea of tantra is that Kundalini, or sexual energy, is a powerful force that may be used to awaken higher states of consciousness and achieve spiritual enlightenment. Practitioners learn to awaken and channel Kundalini energy throughout the body by using methods like tantric breathing, visualization, and energy circulation, which activates dormant spiritual centres called chakras. Through consistent practice, people can transcend the boundaries of the physical world and realize their limitless potential, experiencing moments of pleasure, ecstasy, and spiritual unity.

A potent channel for transforming sexual energy into spiritual development is creative expression. Throughout history, several artists have used the raw energy of sexuality as fuel for their artistic creations. By directing sexual energy towards artistic endeavours like writing, painting, dancing, and music, people can surpass their ego's limitations and access more advanced levels of inspiration and spiritual understanding. People can express themselves, discover more about themselves, enter various states of consciousness, and connect with the divine creative source that is inside of them through the process of creating. Semen retention, also known as sexual continence, is the practice of not ejaculating in order to retain and direct sexual energy for spiritual goals. Sexual continence is seen to improve energy, mental clarity, and spiritual awareness.

It has its roots in a variety of spiritual traditions and esoteric teachings. People who abstain from ejaculation can redirect the powerful energy that is produced during sexual pleasure toward more spiritual activities like prayer, meditation, and introspection. Sexual continence practitioners can develop a stronger bond with their own inner strength and spiritual essence via self-control and discipline. Integration is necessary for the transformation of sexual energy into spiritual development.

Through the integration of creative expression, tantra, sacred sexuality, mindfulness, and sexual continence, people can develop a comprehensive perspective on spiritual development via their sexuality. Every method provides a different way to awaken higher realms of consciousness and access the transforming potential of sexual energy. Embracing these techniques as novices in the field of erotic wizardry can result in tremendous revelations, release, and a greater comprehension of the innate relationship between spirituality and sexuality. In summary, the transformation of sexual energy into spiritual development signifies a deep path toward enlightenment, empowerment, and self-discovery.

Through the investigation and assimilation of several methodologies grounded on mindfulness, tantra, sacred sexuality, artistic expression, and sexual continence, people can unleash the metamorphic possibilities of their sexuality and commence a journey towards spiritual advancement and satisfying pleasure. Exploring sexual energy becomes a sacred adventure for self-realization and divine union in the world of erotic wizardry. This path leads to profound revelations, liberation, and the awakening of one's true essence.

Case studies and examples of successful alchemical practices

The field of alchemy, which is sometimes perceived as mystical and esoteric, offers the possibility of spiritual advancement and metamorphosis. Within the framework of erotic wizardry, alchemical activities provide access to our sexual energy's hidden potential, which can be used for enlightenment and personal development. Numerous case studies and instances of people who have effectively transformed their sexual energy into higher states of awareness and spiritual realization over the years are available. Here, we look at a few of these incredible tales and the lessons they might teach newcomers starting out on their own sexual alchemical path. The Taoist doctrine of sexual cultivation is one of the best-known instances of effective alchemical practice. A complex system of sexual rituals was created by Taoist sages in ancient China with the intention of utilizing the body's Qi, or life force, and distributing it throughout the body for longevity, well-being, and spiritual enlightenment.

The "Secret of the Golden Flower," which outlines numerous methods for channelling sexual energy toward the advancement of consciousness, is one of the core texts of Taoist sexual alchemy. Practitioners learn to cultivate a harmonious balance of Yin and Yang energies and awaken the body's dormant energy centres through techniques like the Inner Smile and the Microcosmic Orbit. Achieving great clarity, vitality, and spiritual realization, Taoist adepts harmonize their sexual energy with the natural rhythms of the world.

The Western alchemist tradition, whose adherents attempted to turn base metals into gold as a symbol for spiritual transformation, provides another noteworthy case study. Inner alchemy was portrayed in the writings of famous alchemists like Carl Jung and Paracelsus as a process of self-integration and self-discovery. The symbolism of alchemical imagery was studied by Jung, in particular, as a metaphor for the individuation process, which is the path towards completeness and the fusion of the conscious and unconscious parts of the mind. Jung explained in his books how the psychological processes of breakdown, purification, and rebirth are linked to the alchemical stages of nigredo (blackening), albedo (whitening), and rubedo (reddening). People may do their own inner alchemical labour, turning the raw material of their unconscious desires and fears into the gold of spiritual realization by engaging in introspection, dream analysis, and active imagination. With its origins in ancient Indian teachings, kundalini yoga focuses on awakening the dormant spiritual force at the base of your spine and channelling it upwards via the energy centres to attain enlightenment.

Many people envision the energy known as Kundalini as a coiled serpent lying resting at the foundation of the spine, waiting to be aroused by various yoga techniques such as pranayama, meditation, and asana. Practitioners may go into deep realms of joy, ecstasy, and spiritual awakening as the Kundalini energy rises. On the other hand, Kundalini awakening can also be a turbulent and challenging process that needs inner cleansing, discipline, and guidance. States of spiritual revelation and unity with the divine can be attained by individuals with dedicated effort and commitment to the transformational power of Kundalini. Apart from these case studies from history and culture, there are also examples from the present day of people who have effectively incorporated alchemical concepts into their erotic practices. The work of contemporary Tantra teachers, who provide seminars and retreats focused on examining the junction of sexuality and spirituality, is one example of this kind of activity. By combining contemporary psychological concepts and physical methods with classic Tantric teachings, these experts provide a secure and encouraging atmosphere where people can explore their genital energy and its potential for personal growth.

Through techniques like breathwork, ritual, and conscious touch, participants discover how to develop a stronger bond with both themselves and their partners and unleash the life-changing potential of erotic alchemy. To sum up, the case studies and illustrations of effective alchemical techniques offer beginners starting out on their own path of erotic magic insightful information and motivation. These tales show the transformational power of using sexual energy for enlightenment and spiritual progress, whether they are taken from modern Tantra teachings or from older traditions like Taoist sexual cultivation, Kundalini yoga, or Western alchemy. People can uncover the mysteries of their sexuality and start along a journey of profound self-discovery, healing, and transformation by devoting themselves to the exploration of these practices with openness, curiosity, and determination.

CHAPTER IV

The Enchantment of Tantric Practices

Introduction to tantric rituals and their significance in erotic wizardry

Tantra, a long-standing spiritual practice with roots in the Indian subcontinent, provides a profoundly transformational perspective on both sexuality and spirituality. The core idea of Tantric philosophy is that there are routes to spiritual enlightenment and divine realization that can be taken via any part of life, including the physical body and sensual experiences. Tantra is essential in the field of erotic wizardry because it offers a framework for directing and using sexual energy for healing, spiritual enlightenment, and personal development. This article provides an overview of Tantric rituals and their importance in the practice of erotic wizardry, providing newcomers with information and direction as they begin this sacred path of self-realization and empowerment.

Rituals aimed at reawakening and igniting the body's latent Kundalini energies are the foundation of Tantric practice. The primordial life force energy that forms the basis of all existence is symbolized by Kundalini, who is frequently pictured as a coiled serpent resting at the base of the spine. The goal of Tantric rituals is to guide this dormant Kundalini energy upward via the chakras toward spiritual illumination and oneness with the divine by waking it up and raising it. Tantric practices frequently include breathing exercises, visualization, mantra chanting, meditation, and sacred sexuality with the intention of balancing and harmonizing the energies of the body, mind, and spirit. Cultivating awareness and presence in each instant is one of the central tenets of

Tantric practices. Tantric practitioners consider every moment as a chance for spiritual communion and transformation, and they approach their rituals with a feeling of reverence, intentionality, and awareness.

Through practising awareness during Tantric rituals, people can experience tremendous experiences of ecstasy, happiness, and spiritual union while strengthening their bonds with the divine, themselves, and their companions. Practitioners can feel more significant levels of intimacy and connection during their rituals by learning to heighten their sensitivity to subtle energy flows within the body via techniques like mindful touch and conscious breathing. Another essential component of Tantric rituals is sacred sexuality, which highlights the close relationship between sexuality and spirituality.

Tantra views sexual energy as a potent force that can be used for spiritual awakening, personal development, and healing. People who participate in Tantric rituals learn to approach sex with intention and reverence, seeing it as a holy act of unity and communion with the divine. In addition to helping couples become more intimate and connected, tantric practices like conscious lovemaking, tantric massage, and energy exchange techniques help awaken and channel the powerful energy of sexual desire toward higher states of awareness and spiritual experience. Tantric rituals frequently employ symbols and ritual objects to promote spiritual awareness and transformation. These items, which aid in channeling and directing the flow of energy within the ritual area, include yantras (geometric diagrams), murtis (holy pictures), and ritual instruments. They also serve as focus places for concentration and meditation. Tantric symbols, including the lingam and yoni, stand for the universe's creative force as well as the fusion of feminine and masculine energy. Tantric practitioners can harness the transformational power of these symbols and harmonize with the divine energies of creation and manifestation by meditating on them during rituals. In addition, mantras—sacred sounds or chants—are frequently used in Tantric ceremonies to call upon particular energies and deities.

It is said that mantras have the ability to alter consciousness and elicit states of acute awareness and enlightenment. During Tantric ceremonies, practitioners can connect with the divine vibrations of the universe by chanting mantras, which can help activate Kundalini energy and lead to spiritual illumination. Depending on the particular goal and emphasis of the ceremony, mantras might be sung softly, loudly, alone, or in groups. To sum up, tantric rituals are essential to the practice of erotic magic because they provide a profound and revolutionary perspective on spirituality and sexuality. By means of rituals that are intended to activate Kundalini energy, develop mindfulness and presence, harness sacred sexuality, and call upon divine energies through symbols and mantras, practitioners can access the latent potential within themselves and unleash the transformative potential of sexual energy for spiritual awakening and personal development. Adopting Tantric rituals can help those who are new to the world of sensual wizardry achieve great insights, healing, and the awakening of their inner divinity.

Exploring sacred sexuality and its role in spiritual connection

Throughout history, many different spiritual traditions have honoured and investigated sacred sexuality, which is a profound and age-old practice. It includes the notion that becoming sexually active can be a holy and life-changing event that opens doors to increased intimacy, spirituality, and self-awareness. Sacred sexuality is essential to the field of erotic wizardry because it provides practitioners with a paradigm for using sexual energy to promote healing, spiritual development, and oneness with the divine. Here, we explore sacred sexuality and how important it is for spiritual awakening and connection. We also offer advice and insights to those who are just starting out on this sacred path of self-awareness and change. Sacred sexuality is fundamentally about treating sex with honour, purpose, and awareness, seeing it as a sacred act of unity and communion with the divine. Sacred sexuality encourages people to regard sex as a means of spiritual development and connection, in contrast to traditional beliefs that see it as solely a physical or recreational activity.

Through the practice of bringing consciousness and presence to every sexual moment, practitioners can experience tremendous feelings of ecstasy, happiness, and spiritual union while strengthening their connection to the divine, themselves, and their partners. In order to transcend the limitations of the ego and access the limitless supply of love and energy within, people can learn to cultivate a deeper sense of intimacy and connection during their sexual encounters by engaging in practices like energy exchange techniques, tantric massage, and conscious breathing. Recognizing the divine nature of the body and its potential for pleasure and ecstasy is one of the key tenets of sacred sexuality.

Many spiritual traditions consider sexual energy as a holy gift that should be cherished and revered and the body as a temple of the divine. Practitioners can develop a greater feeling of self-love and acceptance by accepting their bodies and all of their sensory pleasures, which can lead to intense experiences of joy, contentment, and pleasure. People can learn to surrender to the flow of sexual energy inside them and allow it to lead them into states of heightened consciousness and spiritual connection through techniques like sensual touch, erotic massage, and conscious lovemaking. Sacred sexuality also highlights the significance of lovers' energy exchanges and connections. Tantric traditions hold that sexual energy is a powerful force that may be guided and tapped into for healing and spiritual awakening. Partners can learn to coordinate their energy fields and unite their consciousnesses through practices like eye gazing, breath work, and energy circulation exercises, which will create a deep sense of intimacy and connection. A profound sense of unity and connection with one another as well as the divine is made possible by this energy exchange, which also dissolves ego boundaries and permits the sharing and exploration of pleasure between the parties. Furthermore, holy sexuality promotes the integration of both the feminine and male energies inside each person, as well as the study of the entire range of human sexuality. The unification of feminine and masculine energy is interpreted in many spiritual traditions as a metaphor for the unification of opposites within the self and the universe. People can develop a sense of wholeness, integration, and spiritual empowerment by learning to balance and reconcile these polarities within themselves through activities like Kundalini yoga and Taoist sexual cultivation.

Through the acceptance and celebration of their dual nature, practitioners can access the more profound aspects of their sexuality and unleash the transformational potential of sexual energy for spiritual and personal development. Moreover, holy sexuality encourages people to view sexual relations as a type of spiritual exercise and incorporate it into their everyday lives in order to strengthen their bond with the divine. Practitioners can learn to infuse their sexual interactions with intention, attention, and reverence, turning them into holy rituals of connection and oneness with the divine by developing a regular practice of sacred sexuality. Sacred sexuality, whether pursued alone or in partnership, provides a route to spiritual awakening, healing, and connection. It enables people to access their own limitless supply of love and energy and to sense the divine presence in all facets of their lives.

To sum up, holy sexuality is a powerful and transforming practice that has the capacity to enhance intimacy, spiritual connection, and self-realization. Practitioners can utilize the power of sexual energy to develop spiritual growth, healing, and unity with the divine by approaching sex with reverence, intentionality, and mindfulness. People can discover the mysteries of their sexuality and access their own limitless supply of love and energy by engaging in techniques like conscious breathing, energetic exchange, and the fusion of masculine and feminine energies. For those who are new to the world of erotic wizardry, embracing sacred sexuality can result in healing, awakening the divine within, and deep discoveries.

Step-by-step guide to beginner tantric exercises

Tantra journeying offers people the chance to discover the depths of their sexuality and connect with their inner divine essence. It may be a profound and life-changing experience as novices in the field of erotic magic, understanding and engaging in basic tantric exercises can work as a springboard for discovering the secrets of sexual energy and utilizing it for healing, spiritual awakening, and personal development. Here, we provide a step-by-step tutorial on basic tantric exercises, providing wisdom and direction to individuals starting this holy path of self-realization and empowerment. First, create a sacred space.

Set aside a sacred area to start your tantric practice.

Select a peaceful, cosy space where you feel secure and at ease. Remove all distractions from the area and create a cosy atmosphere with candles, incense, or dim lighting.

To raise the room's spiritual vibrations, you might also want to make an altar out of holy items like flowers, crystals, or pictures of deities. Grounding and centring in step two. Before starting your tantric practice, give yourself a few moments to centre and ground yourself. Either lie down on your back with your arms by your sides or take a comfortable position with your legs crossed. Shut your eyes and exhale deeply through your nose, then slowly exhale through your mouth for several deep breaths. With every breath, visualize roots growing from the base of your spine, firmly anchoring you to the earth. Feel your body becoming more relaxed.

Step 1: Establishing Contact with Your Spouse (if Relevant) If you are doing tantric exercises with a partner, spend some time getting to know each other deeply. Take a comfortable seat facing one another and look directly into each other's eyes. Take turns sharing your goals for the practice, as well as any restrictions or wishes you may have. To connect emotionally and synchronize your breathing, hold hands or place your palms on each other's hearts.

Step 2: Perking Up Your Senses. To increase your awareness and sensation of present-moment presence, use your senses. Start by bringing your attention to your sense of touch and moving your hands mindfully over your body or the body of your partner. Take note of the feel of the skin, the sense of touch, and the movement of energy between you. Go on to your sense of smell now. Inhale deeply and relish the fragrance emanating from the candles or incense. Permit the fragrance to enhance your feelings of ease and transparency. As you continue to fully immerse yourself in the sensory experience of the moment, explore your senses one by one, starting with taste, sound, and sight. Tantric Breathwork,

Step 3: To awaken and circulate the flow of energy within your body, practice tantric breathwork. Begin by taking a slow, deep inhale through your nose. As you do so, feel your belly grow and constrict. Imagine a stream of energy filling your entire body with light and vigour as you breathe, rising from the base of your spine to the top of your head. Envision taking a breath and pulling energy up from the earth; envision exhaling and letting go of any stress or obstructions in your body.

Step 4: Activation of Chakras Pay attention to balancing and opening your body's chakras or energy centres. Start at the base of your spine and see the root chakra filled with a bright red light. Imagine the light becoming more colourful and more vibrant with each breath, firmly rooted in the earth. As you proceed up through the seven chakras, picture a rainbow, with each colour representing a different energy centre. Spend some time establishing a connection with each chakra and letting go of any repressed feelings.

Step 5: Apply a Tantric Massage, Investigate tantric massage as a way to strengthen your bond and intimacy with your spouse. Start by soaking your hands in warm massage oil and using slow, purposeful strokes to softly caress your partner's body. Use your intuition to direct your touch as you pay attention to places that are tense or resistant. Sending loving energy and purpose into your partner's body during the massage will help them unwind and become receptive to the experience. Throughout the massage, encourage your partner to express their preferences and goals and be open to receiving feedback from them.

Step 6: The Holy Union Lastly, to fully experience tantric joy and strengthen your connection, unite in sacred unity with your lover, if applicable. As you move mindfully and slowly, let your bodies unite to form one. To increase closeness and connection, pay attention to deepening your breath and keeping eye contact. Give yourself over to the energy that moves between you during sex and allow it to lead you into ecstasies and spiritual unity.

Throughout the encounter, keep in mind to be mindful

and, in the now, relish every second of communion and connection with your partner.

To sum up, beginning tantric exercises provide a potent means of discovering the secrets of sexual energy and using it for healing, spiritual awakening, and personal development. People can start to tap into the transformative power of Tantra and set out on a journey of profound self-discovery and empowerment by following this step-by-step guide and embracing the practices of creating sacred space, centring and grounding, connecting with your partner, awakening the senses, practising tantric breathwork, activating the chakras, investigating tantric massage, and coming together in sacred union. Embracing tantric techniques as novices in the field of erotic magic can result in great revelations, healing, and the inner awakening of the divine.

CHAPTER V

Exploring the Magic of Erotic Rituals

Ritualistic practices for deepening intimacy and desire

The study of ritualistic activities in the context of erotic wizardry has enormous potential to strengthen intimacy, spark desire, and foster a close bond between lovers. By drawing on the rich tapestry of symbolism and ceremony, rituals provide a holy framework in which people can recognize and enjoy their sexuality. This allows people to experience heightened sensations of arousal and passion. Ritualistic practices, both from antiquated customs and contemporary adaptations, offer a chance to explore the transformational potential of sexual energy and unveil the mysteries of sexuality. Insights and advice for those looking to improve their sensual experiences and create closer bonds with their relationships are provided as we explore ritualistic techniques for increasing closeness and desire. The understanding that sexual activity is a sacred act with spiritual importance and divine potential is the fundamental component of ceremonial activities. People can establish a sacred space in which to explore and express their most vulnerable and profound desires by approaching sex with reverence, intentionality, and mindfulness.

Rituals provide a systematic framework for people to connect with the divine, themselves, and their partners, so serving as a container for this investigation. Ritualistic activities provide a way to go beyond the ordinary and connect with the limitless source of sensual energy that is inside each of us, whether they are derived from antiquated customs or are sparked by one's own imagination. Building a holy altar honouring love and sexuality is a potent ritualistic technique for increasing closeness and desire. With the addition of symbols, pictures, and items with sentimental value, this altar functions as a centre for couples to commemorate and respect their relationship. To arouse feelings of love, passion, and devotion, objects like candles, flowers, crystals, and spiritual texts might be set on the altar.

Couples who want to strengthen their bond and establish goals for their sex may decide to participate in rituals like lighting candles, saying vows, or saying prayers. Couples can harness the transforming power of ritual to improve connection and desire by infusing their lovemaking with the altar's energy. Sensual touch and massage exploration are other ritualistic techniques for increasing intimacy and desire. A sensual massage fosters closeness, vulnerability, and a sense of trust between lovers by facilitating physical, emotional, and energetic connections. To improve the sensory experience, couples can start by setting up a cosy environment with calming music, soft lighting, and scented oils. Partners can alternately massage one other's body, using slow, purposeful strokes to explore each other's tense and sensitive spots. Couples can generate a deep sense of closeness and desire by paying attention to their partner's emotions and wishes. Erotic storytelling is a powerful ceremonial technique that may be used to enhance closeness and desire, just like sensual touch and massage.

Couples can use the power of their imagination to generate passion and arousal by crafting stories of fantasy and desire. Partners who are willing to be open and vulnerable with one another might take turns disclosing their most private thoughts and wants. When a couple explores their dreams together, they might feel a sense of shared intimacy and excitement that can enhance their bond and boost their desire for one another. Erotic storytelling is a fun and imaginative way for partners to explore their imaginations and wants in a secure and encouraging setting, whether through intimate role-playing situations or whispered confessions in the dark. Moreover, engaging in rituals related to holy sexuality might help couples become closer and more in love. Sacred sexuality rituals, originating from ancient traditions like Tantra and Taoism, provide an organized framework for directing and utilizing sexual energy for spiritual enlightenment and personal development. To strengthen their bond and increase their enjoyment, couples might practice techniques like energy circulation, tantric breathing, and ritualized lovemaking. Couples can achieve deep states of pleasure, bliss, and spiritual unity by opening up to the flow of sexual energy and connecting with the divine essence inside themselves and their partners.

Intimacy, passion, and fulfilment in a relationship can be attained through sacred sexuality rituals, which provide a means of overcoming ego constraints and accessing the boundless potential of sensual energy. Finally, in the field of erotic wizardry, ritualistic activities provide a potent and transformative avenue for intensifying closeness and desire. Couples can use the transforming power of ritual to strengthen their bond and rekindle their passion for one another, whether via the creation of sacred altars, sensual touch and massage, erotic storytelling, or sacred sexuality rituals. Couples can create a sacred space in which to explore and express their most vulnerable and profound needs by approaching sex with reverence, intentionality, and awareness.

An organized framework that allows couples to experience intense feelings of closeness, pleasure, and fulfilment is provided by rituals, which act as a container for this exploration. Embracing ceremonial practices can help newcomers to the field of erotic wizardry experience great revelations, healing, and the awakening of the divine within their connection.

Creating sacred space for erotic exploration

The concept of a holy place is crucial to the area of erotic magic because it offers a secure environment in which individuals can discover and share their sex identities in a way that feels loving, safe, and empowered. Sacred space is a state of being rather than just a place; it's a setting where sensual energy can emerge and where intimacy, desire, and connection can grow. People can access the transforming potential of their sexuality and set off on a path of self-discovery, healing, and empowerment by establishing a holy space for erotic exploration. In order to help those who want to embrace their full sexual potential and solve the enigmas surrounding their sexuality, we will explore the concepts and procedures involved in creating a sacred environment for erotic exploration.

Recognizing sex as a sacred act with spiritual meaning and divine potential is fundamental to creating a sacred environment for sensual exploration. People can transform their sensual encounters into avenues for spiritual enlightenment, personal development, and healing by approaching sex with regard, intention, and attention. This investigation is contained in a sacred space, which offers a disciplined environment in which people can establish connections with the divine, their partners, and themselves. Creating a sacred place for sensual exploration, whether done alone or with a partner, enables people to enjoy and embrace their sexuality as a holy gift that can lead to deep transformation and empowerment. Cultivating attention and mindfulness is one of the fundamental tenets of creating a sacred space for erotic exploration.

People are advised to take some time to cultivate a sense of holiness and reverence for the experience, as well as to set clear intentions for their practice, before partaking in any sensual acts. This could be setting up a ritualized area with candles, incense, and holy items, or it could just be taking a few minutes to meditate or practice deep breathing to help oneself centre and ground. People can fully immerse themselves in the sensation of sensual exploration and access the transformational power of sexual energy by practising mindfulness and presence in the moment. This can help people connect with themselves and their relationships on a deeper level. Creating a sacred space for erotic exploration also involves communicating with oneself and any engaged partners and establishing clear limits. Setting boundaries is crucial to making sure that everyone feels secure, appreciated, and able to freely express their preferences and wishes.

Throughout the exploration process, people are urged to honour and respect each other's limits and to speak honestly and freely about their needs, desires, and boundaries with each other and with themselves. This could entail talking about permission, working out limits, and developing a code word or signal to let others know when boundaries are being crossed. People can establish a sacred space where sensual exploration can occur with openness, honesty, and delight by building a container of trust and mutual respect.

Sacred space for sensual exploration is created in large part by the physical environment, in addition to intentionality and boundaries. People are urged to create a cosy and welcoming environment where they feel at ease, at ease, and free to express themselves completely. This could be building a warm and inviting nest with pillows, blankets, and other sensuous items, or it could entail setting the tone with candles, calming music, and pleasant aromas. People may concentrate entirely on the sensation of sensual exploration without outside interruptions or distractions when they are in a physically distraction-free atmosphere that fosters deeper closeness and connection. People can create a sacred space where they can fully submit to the flow of erotic energy and experience profound sensations of pleasure, connection, and ecstasy by creating a supporting and nurturing environment.

In addition, ritual practice has the potential to strengthen the sense of connection and appreciation for the experience while establishing a sacred space for sensual exploration. Rituals offer a disciplined framework within which people can respect and appreciate their sexuality as a holy gift and a source of divine connection. Rituals are a symbolic representation of purpose and mindfulness. To sanctify the room and create the tone for the exploration to come, rituals may involve lighting candles, saying prayers or affirmations, or performing symbolic acts of purification or consecration. People who practice rituals can strengthen their bonds with the divine, their partners, and themselves by erecting a feeling of ceremonial and holiness around their sensual encounters.

To sum up, establishing a sacred space for erotic inquiry is a potent and healing activity that encourages people to value and embrace their sexuality as a holy gift that can lead to significant personal growth and empowerment. People may create a safe space of mutual respect and trust where erotic exploration can happen in an open, joyful, and authentic way by practising intentionality, mindfulness, and clear communication. By creating a holy space for erotic exploration, people can access the transformational power of sexual energy and go on a path of self-discovery, healing, and empowerment—whether they practice alone or with a partner. Embracing the concepts and methods of creating sacred space as novices in the field of erotic wizardry can result in healing, great insights, and the awakening of the divine within

Incorporating elements of magic and symbolism into lovemaking

Within the field of erotic wizardry, the fusion of lovemaking with magic and symbolism provides a powerful means of intensifying connection, stoking passion, and revealing the secrets of sexual energy.

People can access the power of the subconscious mind, the collective unconscious, and the archetypal realm to enhance their erotic experiences and develop a deeper connection with themselves, their partners, and the divine by incorporating elements of magic and symbolism into their sexual encounters. Here, we go into the ideas and methods of fusing magic and symbolism with lovemaking, providing advice and understanding for individuals who want to embrace their entire sexual expression and discover the limits of their erotic potential.

Recognizing sex as a sacred and transformational act endowed with spiritual importance and divine potential is fundamental to fusing aspects of magic and symbolism into lovemaking. People can transform their sexual encounters into opportunities for spiritual enlightenment, personal development, and healing by approaching lovemaking with regard, intention, and mindfulness. People can access the deeper levels of the psyche and the energetic worlds through the use of magic and symbolism, which enables them to draw on the limitless supply of erotic energy that resides inside each of us.

Using magic and symbolism in romantic relationships, whether one is doing it alone or with a partner, encourages people to respect and appreciate their sexuality as a holy gift and a source of deep transformation and empowerment. The practice of intentionality and mindfulness is one of the fundamentals of fusing magic and symbolism into romantic endeavours. People are urged to create a sense of sacredness and reverence for the experience, as well as to make specific intentions for their practice, before partaking in any sexual activity. This could be setting up a ritualized area with candles, incense, and holy items, or it could just be taking a few minutes to meditate or practice deep breathing to help oneself centre and ground. People can fully immerse themselves in the sensation of making love and access the transformational potential of sexual energy by practising mindfulness and presence in the present. This allows them to strengthen their connections to the divine, themselves, and their partners. Using symbols, imagery, and archetypes to inspire deeper layers of meaning and resonance is a crucial part of fusing magic and symbolism into lovemaking. Since ancient times, people have utilized symbols and imagery to gain access to the archetypal realm and subconscious mind, which allows them to access the universal themes and energies that underpin the human experience. People can add deeper levels of meaning and significance to their sexual encounters by incorporating symbols like the pentagram, lotus flower, or yin-yang symbol into their lovemaking.

This enables them to access the transformative power of the collective unconscious and the archetypal realm. Furthermore, the use of affirmations and visualizations can be a potent technique to enhance the energetic vibrations of the lovemaking process and add elements of magic and symbolism. Positive words or phrases known as affirmations are ones that people can say to themselves or to their partners in order to reaffirm a desired goal or result. People can program their subconscious minds to coincide with their intents and desires and more easily and effectively manifest their desires by utilizing affirmations such as "I am open to receiving pleasure" or "I am connected to the divine through my sexuality." In a similar vein, visions entail conjuring up scenarios or images in the mind that symbolize intended results or experiences. People can better match their energetic frequencies with their intentions and attract and materialize their wishes with more clarity and precision by envisioning scenes of passion, connection, and ecstasy. Using rituals can be a potent method to bring aspects of magic and symbolism to lovemaking and create a feeling of ceremonial and sanctity around the experience, in addition to using symbols, imagery, affirmations, and visualizations. Rituals offer a disciplined framework within which people can respect and appreciate their sexuality as a holy gift and a source of divine connection.

Rituals are a symbolic representation of purpose and mindfulness. Rituals to sanctify the area and establish the mood for the lovemaking to come can include lighting candles, saying prayers or affirmations, or performing symbolic acts of purification or consecration. People who practice rituals can strengthen their bonds with God, their lovers, and themselves by establishing a feeling of formality and holiness around their sexual encounters. Adding magical and symbolic components to romantic relationships can also be a very effective way to communicate and explore the deeper facets of one's own psyche and soul.

Through the use of the unconscious mind's symbolic language, people can gain access to hidden facets of both themselves and their relationships, enabling them to examine and resolve resentments, traumas, and blocks that might be preventing them from completely enjoying life and connecting with others. People can access universal energies and qualities that resonate with their own particular experiences and desires by exploring archetypal themes like goddess, warrior, or lover. This enables them to tap into the transformative power of sexual energy and set out on a journey of self-discovery, healing, and empowerment. In conclusion, using magic and symbolism in romantic relationships is a powerful means of enhancing closeness, stoking passion, and unravelling the secrets of sexual energy. In order to harness the transformational power of their sexuality and develop a stronger bond with the divine, people can enhance their sexual interactions using intentionality, mindfulness, symbolism, images, affirmations, visualizations, and rituals. Embracing the ideas and methods of fusing magic and symbolism into romantic relationships as novices in the field of erotic wizardry can result in profound revelations, healing, and the awakening of the divine within.

CHAPTER VI

Embracing the Divine Feminine and Masculine

Understanding the balance of yin and yang energies in love and desire

Recognizing how the yin and yang forces of desire and love are balanced Comprehending the balance between the two opposing energies is essential for fostering desire, fortifying bonds with others, and discovering the mysteries of sexual energy in the realm of erotic sorcery. The idea of yin and yang, which has its roots in ancient Chinese philosophy, symbolizes the dynamic interaction of opposing but complementary forces in both the universe and ourselves. Yin and yang energies, with their distinct features, attributes, and expressions, materialize as the feminine and masculine principles in the framework of love and desire.

We may harness the transforming potential of sexual energy and develop a stronger bond with both ourselves and our partners by comprehending and balancing these forces inside ourselves and our relationships. In order to help people who want to embrace the fullest of their erotic potential and set out on a path of self-discovery and empowerment, we will be discussing the concepts and practices related to understanding the balance of yin and yang forces in love and desire. Realizing the polarity and interdependence of these forces at their core is essential to comprehending the harmony of yin and yang energies in love and desire.

Rather than being static or fixed ideas, yin and yang are dynamic and flowing forces that are always seeking balance and harmony. Yang is a symbol for the masculine principle, which is aggressive, penetrating, and active, whereas yin is a symbol for the feminine principle, which is gentle, receptive, and nurturing. Yang energy is linked to traits like power, passion, and assertiveness, whereas yin energy is connected to traits like tenderness, intuition, and emotional depth in the context of love and desire. We can embrace the fullest range of our erotic potential and bring harmony and wholeness to our feelings of love and desire by balancing these forces within ourselves and our relationships. The development of consciousness and mindfulness is one of the fundamental ideas in comprehending the harmony of yin and yang forces in love and desire. People are advised to spend some time tuning into their own and their partner's energetic states, observing the minute details of yin and yang energy, before partaking in any sensual activities. This could entail techniques like breathwork, meditation, or body awareness exercises to calm the mind and tune in to the body's subtle energy flows.

A stronger sense of closeness and connection can arise when people practice awareness and mindfulness because they will be more aware of their own needs, wants, and boundaries, as well as those of their partners. The development of harmony and balance inside ourselves is a crucial component of realizing the harmony and balance of yin and yang forces in love and desire. According to conventional Chinese philosophy, yin and yang forces in the body and mind are harmoniously balanced when one is well and in good health. Similar to this, people are urged to develop a balance of yin and yang energies inside themselves in the context of love and desire, accepting both their feminine and masculine features in a way that feels real and powerful.

This could entail engaging in activities like writing, introspection, or artistic expression to examine and incorporate various facets of the self, thus facilitating the emergence of a more comprehensive sense of self-acceptance and wholeness. Furthermore, accepting the interaction of paradoxes and opposites within ourselves and our relationships is necessary to comprehend the yin and yang energy balance in love and desire. The dynamics of love and desire are ever-changing, seeking harmony and balance, just as the yin and yang forces. As people work through the complexity of their own needs and desires, there will undoubtedly be moments of stress, conflict, and imbalance in any intimate relationship. People can develop a deeper awareness of themselves and their partners and foster greater empathy, compassion, and connection by seeing these moments as chances for learning and growth. Furthermore, accepting the yin and yang energies in love and want means being willing to let go and allow our relationships and our own natural flow of energy and desire. People are encouraged to believe in the inherent wisdom of their own bodies and instincts, which allows for a deeper sense of spontaneity, authenticity, and pleasure to emerge, as opposed to trying to control or influence the outcome of our sensual experiences.

This could entail techniques like mindful lovemaking, Taoist sexual cultivation, or tantra, which stress the value of giving in to the present moment and letting the energy of desire and love flow naturally. To sum up, realizing how yin and yang forces are balanced in love and desire is a profound and life-changing exercise that encourages people to embrace all of their sensual potential and develop a closer relationship with God, themselves, and their partners. Through the practice of mindfulness and awareness, yin and yang energy balancing within ourselves, accepting contradictions and their interplay, and letting go of control over the natural flow of energy and desire, people can access the transformative potential of sexual energy and set out on a path of healing, self-discovery, and empowerment. Embracing the concepts and methods of comprehending the harmony of yin and yang energies as novices in the field of erotic wizardry can result in healing, profound insights, and the awakening of the divine within.

Honoring and integrating both aspects within oneself and relationships

Deepening connection, fostering passion, and unravelling the secrets of sexual energy are all made possible by the process of acknowledging and integrating both sides of oneself and relationships in the enthralling voyage of erotic wizardry. There is a dynamic interaction of masculine and feminine energy, commonly known as yin and yang, within every person and every connection.

The opposites of existence—active and passive, forceful and receptive, gentle and strong—are represented by these energies. We can realize the full range of our erotic potential and develop a closer bond with the divine, our lovers, and ourselves by valuing and incorporating both parts of who we are. In order to provide insight and direction for those who want to embrace the depth of their erotic experience and set out on a path of self-discovery and empowerment, we here examine the concepts and practices related to recognizing and integrating both elements within oneself and relationships. Understanding the innate harmony and balance that result from the interaction of masculine and feminine energies is fundamental to respecting and integrating both facets of oneself and relationships. The idea of yin and yang in classical Eastern philosophy stands for the dynamic interaction of opposing yet complementary forces in the cosmos and in each of us. Action, aggressiveness, and strength are connected with yang energy, whereas receptivity, intuition, and caring are associated with yin energy.

Each component offers special gifts and insights into the nature of human sensual expression, making each equally important and useful. A greater sense of intimacy, passion, and connection can be experienced when we cultivate a sense of balance, wholeness, and harmony within ourselves and our relationships by accepting and integrating both parts of who we are. The development of self-awareness and self-acceptance is one of the essential tenets of respecting and integrating both sides of oneself and relationships.

We must first reach a profound level of self-awareness and self-acceptance, embracing every part of our being with love, compassion, and understanding before we can genuinely honour and integrate both elements of ourselves. In order to investigate and appreciate the various facets of our male and feminine energies, as well as any conditioning or cultural expectations that may be influencing our perspective of ourselves and our relationships, this may require engaging in activities like meditation, writing, or self-reflection. We can build a basis of honesty and wholeness from which to investigate and integrate both erotic elements of our nature by practising self-awareness and self-acceptance.

The development of harmony and balance between the masculine and feminine energies is a crucial component of respecting and integrating both sides of oneself and interpersonal connections. It can be simple to exhibit masculine and feminine traits in an unbalanced way in a society that frequently prioritizes one over the other. This can cause emotions of alienation, bewilderment, or discontent in both our personal and interpersonal connections.

Through the development of harmony and balance between masculine and feminine energies, we can establish a state of balance that facilitates a more fluid and dynamic expression of our sexual nature. In addition to techniques like breathing exercises, artistic expression, and mindful communication, this may entail techniques like conscious communication, respect for one another, and cooperative decision-making in partnerships. We can develop a sense of wholeness and integration that makes it possible to experience love, passion, and connection on a deeper level by accepting both parts of ourselves and our relationships. Furthermore, it takes a desire to embrace the whole spectrum of our erotic expression, including the shadow elements that may be suppressed or concealed, in order to honour and integrate both aspects within oneself and relationships. According to Jungian psychology, the shadow stands for the unconscious parts of ourselves that we have denied or rejected, frequently due to social conditioning, fear, or guilt.

We can reclaim lost pieces of ourselves and build a sense of wholeness and integration that makes it possible to enjoy a greater level of intimacy and connection both inside ourselves and in our relationships by accepting and integrating our shadow aspects. The unconscious patterns and beliefs that can impact our erotic expression may be explored and integrated through techniques like inner child healing, trauma release, and shadow work. We can cultivate an honest and profound feeling of love, desire, and connection by accepting and embracing the light and shadow sides of our erotic nature. Furthermore, a greater sense of closeness and connection can arise when one is prepared to give in to the natural flow of energy and desire, which is a prerequisite for acknowledging and integrating both parts of oneself and relationships. It can be difficult to give in to the erotic energy's natural ebb and flow in a society that frequently places a premium on power and control in relationships, which can result in feelings of annoyance, bitterness, or alienation.

We may cultivate a sense of trust and vulnerability that enables a deeper experience of intimacy and connection inside ourselves and our relationships by giving in to the natural flow of energy and desire. For a more genuine and satisfying sense of love, passion, and connection, this may entail techniques like tantra, Taoist sexual cultivation, or conscious lovemaking to explore and embrace the inherent rhythms of our sensual nature. We can establish a sense of wholeness and integration that makes it possible to experience love, passion, and connection on a deeper level by acknowledging and integrating both parts of ourselves and our relationships. In the case of novices in the field of sexual wizardry, great insights, healing, and the awakening of the divine within might result from accepting the concepts and practices of honouring and integrating both sides within oneself and relationships.

Exercises for connecting with and embodying these energies

Within the field of erotic wizardry, the path of embracing and relating to both male and feminine energies has the capacity to profoundly enhance intimacy, foster desire, and reveal the secrets of sexual energy. People can reach their full sensual potential and establish a sense of harmony, balance, and wholeness in their relationships as well as in themselves by purposefully practising and exercising activities that foster a deeper connection with these energies. In order to help people enjoy the richness of their sensual experience and awaken to the divine within, we explore a range of activities here for connecting with and embodying both male and feminine energies.

Conscious breathing is a useful technique for embodying and establishing a connection with masculine energy. By developing a sense of presence, power, and groundedness inside oneself, conscious breathing enables people to access the traits that are linked with masculine energy, which includes strength, assertiveness, and action. People can start practising conscious breathing by sitting comfortably and inhaling slowly and deeply into their chest, abdomen, and diaphragm. They can picture themselves pulling in strong, forceful, and masculine energy as they inhale, and as they exhale, they can let go of any resistance, tension, or tension, enabling themselves to fully embody the attributes of masculine energy. Sensual movement is a potent practice for expressing and establishing a connection with feminine energy. Sensual movement fosters a sense of flow, grace, and surrender within oneself, which enables people to access traits connected with feminine energy, such as receptivity, intuition, and sensuality.

People can start practising sensuous movement by turning on some sultry, relaxing music and letting their bodies move naturally and freely to the beat of the song. In order to connect with their bodies' inherent knowledge and submit to the natural rhythms of their own feminine energy, they can experiment with soft, flowing motions like swaying, undulating, and whirling. The technique of visualization can be an effective means of establishing a connection with and embodying both feminine and masculine energy, in addition to aware breathing and sensuous movement. Through visualization, people can use their imagination to conjure up vivid scenarios and ideas in their minds that arouse both feminine and male energy within them. To engage in visualization exercises, people should locate a peaceful, comfortable area, close their eyes, and allow themselves to sink into a deeply relaxed and open condition. Then, by allowing oneself to fully immerse in the experience and feel the energies flowing through them, one can envision themselves embodying the attributes of masculine and feminine energy—soft, nurturing, and receptive to feminine energy, and strong, confident, and forceful for masculine energy. Partner exercises can also be an effective means of embodying and establishing a connection with both masculine as well as feminine energies in the context of a relationship.

Through dynamic and engaging exploration of the interplay of masculine and feminine energy, partner exercises help people develop a closer, more intimate relationship with their partners. Mirroring is one technique that couples can use to connect with masculine energy. In order to coordinate their energy and foster a sense of harmony and connection, couples in this activity stand facing each other and alternately imitate each other's movements, gestures, and expressions. In a similar vein, partners can access their bodies' inherent wisdom and connect with the flow of feminine energy between them by practising techniques like breathwork, eye gazing, or sensual touch to connect with feminine energy. Furthermore, ritual practice can be a potent means of embodying and establishing a connection with both male and feminine energies inside oneself and one's relationships. Rituals are a structured framework that allows people to appreciate and enjoy the attributes of male and feminine energy. Rituals are symbolic manifestations of attention and mindfulness.

For instance, as a means of honouring and connecting with these energies, people can make a ritual altar dedicated to the divine masculine and feminine within themselves, incorporating symbols, images, and objects that represent these energies. They can also engage in practices like lighting candles, reciting prayers or affirmations, or making offerings. In a similar vein, partners can celebrate the interaction of their masculine and feminine energies by developing rituals like date nights, love-making ceremonies, or holy union rites.

These rituals will strengthen their bond and intimacy with one another. To sum up, practices that help one connect to and embody both male and feminine energies provide a potent means of fostering desire, increasing intimacy, and unravelling the secrets of sexual energy inside oneself and one's relationships. People can realize their full erotic potential and establish a sense of harmony, balance, and wholeness in their relationships and themselves by practising techniques like conscious breathing, sensuous movement, visualization, partner exercises, and ritual. Accepting these exercises as novices in the field of erotic wizardry can result in deep realizations, healing, and the divine inside emerging, enabling people to go on a path of self-discovery, empowerment, and metamorphosis.

CHAPTER VII

Navigating Ethical and Responsible Erotic Wizardry

Discussing the importance of consent, boundaries, and ethics in magical practices

One cannot stress the value of permission, boundaries, and ethics in the field of erotic wizardry, where the forces of magic and sexuality converge. All magical practices are based on these tenets, which direct practitioners in their discovery of erotic energy and guarantee that their encounters are secure, courteous, and empowering for all parties. Practitioners can provide a safe space of mutual respect and trust in order to explore the fullest extent of their erotic potential and set out on a path of self- discovery, healing, and transformation by upholding the principles of consent, boundaries, and ethics.

Here, we explore the role that permission, boundaries, and ethics play in magical practices, providing understanding and direction for individuals who want to dance the complex tango of magic and sexuality with honour and integrity. The basic right of individuals to make informed and voluntary decisions regarding their participation in magical or erotic activities is the basis of magical practices, and it is known as the consent principle. Getting consent is not the only thing that consent entails. It also involves respecting each person's autonomy, agency, and dignity, as well as making sure that their limits and desires are honoured.

In the context of magical practices, consent necessitates mutual awareness of each participant's intentions, wants, and boundaries, as well as clear and unambiguous communication between all parties. Throughout any magical or erotic activity, practitioners are advised to get enthusiastic and continuing consent. They should also check in with themselves and their partners on a frequent basis to make sure that everyone feels safe, respected, and free to express their preferences and wishes. Another crucial component of magical practices is boundaries, which provide a secure, supportive, and empowering environment for people to explore and express their erotic energy. Each person has personal boundaries that are distinct to them; these boundaries serve as the upper bounds of what they consider to be acceptable, safe, and comfortable in a particular circumstance.

Within the framework of magical practices, practitioners are urged to clearly and assertively define and explain their boundaries, respecting others' boundaries while also recognizing their own needs, desires, and limitations. Setting boundaries—physical, emotional, or energetic—as well as creating guidelines and agreements for consent and communication in the magical realm may all be part of this. Practitioners can establish a safe space of mutual respect and trust in order to explore and express their erotic energy with integrity and authenticity by honouring and respecting each other's boundaries. In order to guarantee that practitioners' acts are consistent with their beliefs, goals, and objectives, ethics serve as the guiding principles that direct their moral and ethical behaviour in their magical activities. Ethical considerations in the context of magical activities cover a broad spectrum of matters, including accountability, honesty, transparency, and integrity. It is recommended that practitioners develop a strong sense of ethical awareness and responsibility, making thoughtful decisions that demonstrate their dedication to upholding the dignity and well-being of all involved beings.

This could be following moral codes, ethical standards, or community norms. It could also entail continuing introspection, self-study, and self-improvement to enhance their comprehension of ethical concepts and how they apply them to their magical endeavours. Practitioners can establish a culture of trust, safety, and empowerment within the magical community by living ethical values like respect, compassion, and integrity. This will help to create an atmosphere where everyone feels respected, valued, and supported on their path to self-discovery and transformation. Moreover, consent, limits, and ethics are crucial not only for specific magical acts but also for the larger social and cultural contexts in which they are performed. Practitioners are called upon to challenge and modify toxic attitudes and beliefs about consent, sexuality, and power dynamics in a society that frequently reinforces them.

They advocate for increased awareness, education, and accountability both inside and outside of the magical community. This could entail actively supporting campaigns and groups that advance social justice, diversity, and inclusivity within the magical community, as well as taking part in talks, workshops, or trainings on subjects like consent culture, trauma-informed practice, and ethical leadership. Practitioners can aid in the destruction of oppressive systems and the creation of a more just and empowered environment for all creatures by cooperating to establish a culture of consent, boundaries, and ethics.

To sum up, the cornerstones of magical practices are permission, boundaries, and ethics. These principles let practitioners explore erotic energy and make sure that their experiences are safe, respectful, and empowering for all parties. Practitioners can provide a safe space of mutual respect and trust in which to explore the fullest extent of their erotic potential and set off on a path of self-discovery, healing, and transformation by upholding these values with integrity. As novices in the field of erotic wizardry, accepting the significance of consent, limits, and ethics can result in deep realizations, healing, and the inner awakening of the divine, enabling people to dance the complex dance between magic and sexuality with honour, sincerity, and respect.

Addressing common misconceptions and pitfalls

Practitioners may run into a number of myths and traps in the ethereal world of erotic wizardry, where magic and sexuality converge, which might impede their path to self- realization, empowerment, and change. These myths and traps are frequently brought about by cultural taboos, societal conditioning, and a lack of knowledge about erotic energy and its potential for development and healing. Practitioners can move more confidently, honourably, and reverently over the complex terrain of erotic wizardry by clearly and mindfully confronting these myths and traps. Here, we examine some of the widespread myths and traps surrounding erotic wizardry and provide advice and ideas for anyone looking to set out on a voyage of self-discovery. A prevalent misperception in the field of sexual wizardry is the notion that magic and sex are intrinsically opposed and incompatible realms. As it happens, sex and magic have always been linked, with many traditions and rituals acknowledging the transformational potential of sensual energy for human development and spiritual advancement. Practitioners can access a tremendous pool of erotic energy within themselves and use it for healing, manifestation, and spiritual enlightenment by accepting the connection between sex and magic.

However, in order to ensure that these practices are carried out with permission, respect, and integrity, it is crucial to approach the merger of sex and magic with mindfulness, intentionality, and ethical awareness. The idea that erotic wizardry is only about getting arousal or sexual fulfilment is another widespread fallacy. Although enjoyment and satisfaction are crucial components of erotic magic, they are but one facet of a deeper, more comprehensive path of self-realization and empowerment. Sacred sexuality, Taoist sexual cultivation, tantra, and sexual shamanism are just a few of the practices and disciplines that fall under the umbrella of "erotic wizardry." Each of these approaches offers a different way to delve into the depths of erotic energy and discover how it can be used for spiritual awakening, healing, and transformation. Practitioners can go on a path of investigation and discovery that goes beyond simple physical pleasure and opens the door to significant discoveries, healing, and transformation by accepting the complex nature of erotic wizardry. The propensity to idealize or romanticize particular customs or acts without fully comprehending their cultural context or associated consequences is a typical mistake in erotic magic. For instance, tantra, a spiritual and philosophical practice that has its roots in ancient India, has sometimes been misunderstood and sold in Western culture as a quick fix for developing numerous orgasms or sexual prowess.

True tantra, however, is a comprehensive system of spiritual practice that includes meditation, breathwork, visualization, ritual, and much more than just sexual techniques. Its goals are to awaken the divine within and foster a closer relationship with oneself, one's partner, and the universe. Tantra practitioners can embrace the full depth and richness of this age-old wisdom and avoid the traps of superficiality and exploitation by approaching the practice with humility, reverence, and a readiness to learn from genuine teachers and lineages. Prioritizing success and performance over presence and genuineness during sexual interactions is another frequent mistake.

People may feel under pressure to perform or live up to expectations in a culture that frequently exalts sexual prowess and performance. This can result in feelings of inadequacy, alienation, or uneasiness over their sexual encounters. True erotic wizardry, however, is about fostering presence, sincerity, and vulnerability in the moment and allowing oneself to fully inhabit the depths of sensual energy within; it has nothing to do with impressing others or reaching a certain goal. In order to experience erotic energy more authentically and fulfillingly and to fully realize its transformational potential, practitioners can establish a space of trust, intimacy, and connection within themselves and their relationships by letting go of expectations, judgments, and comparisons. In addition, it is critical to dispel the myth that erotic magic is exclusive to a small group of people or that obtaining these skills requires a particular set of credentials. In actuality, everyone has the innate ability to perform erotic wizardry, regardless of their age, gender, sexual preference, or degree of expertise. Every individual has the ability to investigate and utilize the transformational potential of erotic energy for recovery, development, and spiritual enlightenment. Through acceptance of this reality and an open-minded, curious, and learning-focused attitude to erotic wizardry, practitioners can set off on a personal and unique path of self-exploration and empowerment.

In conclusion, in order for practitioners of erotic wizardry to navigate the complex terrain of sexual energy with integrity, sincerity, and reverence, it is imperative that they confront frequent misconceptions and mistakes. Practitioners can go on a journey of exploration and discovery that results in profound insights, healing, and transformation by acknowledging the connection between sex and magic, embracing the multifaceted nature of erotic wizardry, approaching practices with mindfulness and ethical awareness, valuing presence and authenticity over performance, and embracing the accessibility of erotic wizardry to all individuals. Accepting these guidelines as novices in the field of erotic wizardry can help one gain a better awareness of who they are, what they want, and the limitless possibilities of erotic energy for development, healing, and spiritual awakening.

Guidelines for ethical engagement in love and desire magic

Practitioners of sexual wizardry are expected to approach their trade with integrity, respect, and ethical awareness in the mysterious world where the energies of love and desire entwine with the secrets of magic. While there is great potential for transformation, healing, and spiritual development in love and desire magic, it also comes with a responsibility to make sure that our practices are carried out with the greatest moral standards and good intentions. Practitioners can negotiate the complexity of their craft with integrity and reverence by abiding by the rules for ethical involvement in love and desire magic. This creates a container of trust and empowerment that allows them to explore the depths of their erotic potential. Here, we examine some of the fundamental rules for morally responsible love and desire magic, providing wisdom and direction for anyone looking to set out on a path of self-discovery. First and foremost, adherence to the consent principle is necessary for moral participation in love and desire magic. All magical practices are based on consent, which guarantees that everyone involved in magical or sensual actions is fully informed and willing to participate. In order to guarantee that everyone feels comfortable, respected, and empowered to freely express their desires and boundaries, practitioners are recommended to get clear and unambiguous consent from all persons involved.

In order to enable a shared understanding of goals, desires, and boundaries, this may entail practitioners and their partners engaging in continuous discourse, active listening, and open and honest communication. Love and desire magicians may foster an environment of empowerment and trust where people feel free to explore and express their erotic potential in a respectful and ethical manner by emphasizing consent. The idea of non-coercion is another crucial rule for moral love and desire magic work. Coercion is the practice of forcing someone against their will to engage in magical or sensual practices using coercion, pressure, or force. In their magical activities, practitioners are advised to avoid coercive methods and strategies in favour of creating an atmosphere of autonomy, respect, and trust where everyone feels free to make their own decisions. This could entail recognizing others' limits and boundaries, upholding their autonomy and agency, and abstaining from actions that could endanger or distress others. Practitioners can cultivate a culture of consent and empowerment within the magical community by upholding the principle of non-coercion. This will enable everyone to feel respected, appreciated, and supported as they embark on their journey of self-discovery. Furthermore, an ethical commitment to openness and truthfulness is necessary for engaging in love and desire magic.

In order to create a safe space where clients can explore and express their erotic potential, practitioners are urged to be forthright and honest with both clients and partners about their goals, desires, and boundaries. This could entail having candid conversations, sharing one's ideas, emotions, and also experiences in an honest and open manner, and being prepared to listen and react in a kind and understanding manner. In love and want magic, practitioners can foster an environment of integrity and authenticity where everyone feels heard, seen, and respected on their path to self-realization and strength by emphasizing openness and truth. Furthermore, a dedication to honesty and responsibility is necessary for moral participation in love and desire magic. It is recommended that practitioners behave honourably when engaging in magical activities, making sure their deeds reflect their beliefs, goals, and aspirations and accepting accountability for the results of their decisions. To further comprehend ethical concepts and how they apply to magical activities, one may need to engage in constant self-reflection, self-inquiry, and self-improvement.

One may also need to be prepared to hold oneself and others accountable for any harm or wrongdoing that may arise. Within the magical community, practitioners can cultivate an atmosphere of trust, respect, and empowerment by modelling integrity and accountability in love and desire magic. This will enable everyone to feel encouraged and empowered to explore and express their erotic potential with reverence and integrity. Moreover, adhering to the damage reduction principle is necessary for moral participation in love and desire magic. By taking proactive steps to reduce the dangers and harms that may be connected to magical or sensual practices, harm reduction aims to make sure that everyone involved feels secure, respected, and supported as they embark on their path of exploration and discovery. It is advised that practitioners weigh the advantages and disadvantages of any magical practices they partake in, considering aspects like energetic, emotional, and bodily safety as well as any effects on others and oneself. This could entail establishing precise guidelines and rules for consent and communication, as well as being ready to step in and offer help if something hurts or uncomfortable happens.

Love and desire magicians may foster a culture of safety, respect, and empowerment where everyone feels free to explore and express their erotic potential with courage and honesty by emphasizing harm prevention above all else. To sum up, in order for practitioners to traverse the difficulties of their trade with integrity, respect, and reverence, ethical engagement in love and desire magic is vital. Through adherence to established protocols for consent, non-coercion, transparency, honesty, integrity, responsibility, and harm reduction, practitioners can establish a secure and empowering environment in which individuals can respectfully and honourably explore and express their erotic potential. Adopting these rules as novices in the field of erotic wizardry can result in deep realizations, healing, and transformation. This will enable practitioners to move confidently, authentically, and reverently over the complex terrain of love and desire magic.

CHAPTER VIII

Overcoming Challenges and Obstacles

Strategies for overcoming blocks and obstacles on the path of erotic wizardry

Practitioners of sexual wizardry may run into a number of roadblocks and impediments on their magical journey that obstruct their route to empowerment, change, and self-discovery. These roadblocks and impediments frequently result from both external (such as cultural indoctrination or taboos in society) and internal (such as guilt, fear, or limiting beliefs) hurdles. Nonetheless, practitioners can unlock the full potential of their erotic journey by using tactics for overcoming these roadblocks and hurdles and navigating the complex terrain of erotic energy with perseverance, courage, and honesty.

Here, we look at some of the most important techniques for getting past roadblocks and hurdles in the pursuit of erotic wizardry, providing advice and insights for anyone looking to set off on a voyage of self-discovery. In the realm of erotic magic, practising self-awareness and self-reflection is one of the best ways to get beyond roadblocks and barriers. Cultivating a profound understanding of oneself, including thoughts, feelings, desires, and fears, is the goal of self-awareness. On the other hand, self-reflection entails looking at the habits, beliefs, and behaviours that can be causing roadblocks and hurdles in one's erotic journey. It is recommended that practitioners investigate their inner landscape and identify any unconscious hurdles or limits that might be impeding them by practising mindfulness, writing, or therapy. Practitioners can start to remove the constraints and hurdles preventing them from realizing their full erotic potential by lighting the light of awareness on their inner world. This will enable a stronger sense of empowerment, authenticity, and freedom to surface. In erotic magic, practising self-acceptance and self-compassion is another effective way to get beyond roadblocks. Regarding their erotic experiences or urges, many practitioners may harbour deep-seated shame or guilt, which can result in feelings of inadequacy, unworthiness, or self-judgment. However, practitioners can learn to embrace themselves with kindness, understanding, and forgiveness by practising self-compassion and self-acceptance. They will realize that they are naturally deserving of love and acceptance, regardless of their prior experiences or apparent inadequacies. A deeper sense of integration and completeness can arise by nurturing and healing the damaged parts of oneself through techniques like inner child work, self-care, and affirmations.

Through the process of accepting and loving oneself, practitioners can start to let go of any guilt or shame that could be preventing them from experiencing erotic fulfilment. This will enable them to express their erotic nature in a more genuine and free way. Practitioners can gain from the support and direction of mentors and the community, in addition to self-awareness and self-compassion, as they work to overcome roadblocks and hurdles in erotic magic.

Mentors offer knowledge, direction, and encouragement to help practitioners overcome their limitations and realize their full potential, while communities offer a sense of validation, support, and belonging that may be extremely helpful in navigating the difficulties and uncertainties of the sexual journey. It is recommended that practitioners look for communities and persons who share their beliefs and goals, as well as mentors or teachers who have been there before and can provide advice and support along the journey. On their path to erotic wizardry, practitioners can develop the bravery, fortitude, and perseverance necessary to go beyond roadblocks and hurdles by surrounding themselves with a supportive group and asking mentors for advice. In addition, practitioners can utilize a range of strategies and tactics to target particular roadblocks and hindrances that might be preventing them from reaching their goal of erotic fulfilment.

For instance, body acceptance, self-love, or erotic embodiment practices can help practitioners who are experiencing problems with their bodies or poor self-esteem reestablish a deeper sense of acceptance and worth for their bodies. In order to build the confidence and assertiveness required to assert their needs and desires authentically, practitioners who find it difficult to communicate their desires or set boundaries may find it helpful to engage in practices like assertiveness training, communication skills, or boundary-setting exercises. Practitioners can transcend their limitations and unleash the full potential of their erotic energy, enabling a more meaningful and empowered experience of love, desire, and intimacy. This is achieved by pinpointing the specific blocks and obstacles that are present in their erotic journey and using focused techniques and practices to address them.

To sum up, conquering roadblocks and hindrances on the way to erotic magic is a crucial part of the process of self-awareness, empowerment, and metamorphosis. In order to unlock the full potential of their erotic energy and experience a deeper sense of fulfilment, connection, and empowerment, practitioners can navigate the challenges and uncertainties of the erotic journey with resilience, courage, and authenticity by utilizing strategies like self-awareness and self-reflection, self-compassion and self-acceptance, community and mentorship, and targeted techniques and practices. Adopting these techniques as novices in the field of erotic wizardry can result in deep realizations, healing, and transformation, enabling practitioners to move confidently, honourably, and reverently through the complex terrain of sensual energy.

Dealing with societal conditioning and stigma surrounding sexuality

Practitioners of erotic wizardry frequently face the difficult obstacle of social conditioning and the stigma associated with sexuality. People are exposed to messages and ideas about sex and desire from an early age that are frequently laced with fear, shame, and false information. It can be quite difficult to completely explore and embrace one's erotic nature because of these cultural standards and attitudes. Nonetheless, practitioners can recover their power, free themselves from restrictive ideas, and set out on a path of self-discovery, empowerment, and transformation by comprehending and overcoming the effects of societal conditioning and stigma. Here, we look at some of the ways that stigma and cultural conditioning show up and provide advice on how to overcome them while pursuing erotic wizardry. The constant instillation of guilt and shame is one of the most widespread examples of cultural conditioning related to sexuality. People are frequently indoctrinated from an early age that sex and desire are shameful or evil, which causes them to feel inadequate or guilty about their sensual experiences and wants. This shame-based conditioning can have a profound effect on one's sense of belonging, worth, and self-esteem. As a result, it may be challenging to explore and express one's erotic side honestly.

In order to replace shame-based attitudes and ideas that have been internalized as a result of societal conditioning, practitioners are urged to identify them, confront them, and replace them with a sense of strength, self-acceptance, and love. To achieve a more genuine and free expression of sexuality, this may entail practising self-compassion, self-forgiveness, and erotic embodiment.

These practices can help one develop a deeper sense of connection to and acceptance of their erotic self. The continued reinforcement of binary and heteronormative norms is another prevalent method of social conditioning related to sexuality. What is deemed "normal" or "acceptable" in terms of sexual orientation, gender identity, and also expression is defined narrowly and rigidly in many societies. For those who do not fit into these specific categories, this can pose serious obstacles and result in feelings of guilt, isolation, or invisibility. By accepting a more expansive and inclusive perspective of sexuality that recognizes the diversity and complexity of the human experience, practitioners are encouraged to resist these binary and heteronormative conventions.

This could entail becoming knowledgeable about the range of gender identities, sexual orientations, and expressions, as well as actively promoting the rights and visibility of underrepresented groups in society at large. Inside the field of erotic wizardry, practitioners can cultivate an atmosphere where everyone feels appreciated, respected, and supported in their path toward self-discovery and empowerment by questioning binary and heteronormative norms and promoting an inclusive, diverse, and accepting culture.

Furthermore, negative attitudes and ideas about authority, permission, and limits are frequently reinforced by cultural conditioning related to sexuality. People may feel under pressure to fit into specific roles or expectations during sexual encounters in a culture that frequently praises sexual conquest and dominance. This can result in emotions of coercion, manipulation, or disempowerment. Similar to this, cultural conditioning may also support false beliefs and myths regarding boundaries and consent, which can cause misunderstandings about appropriate and healthy sexual behaviour. It is recommended that practitioners prioritize the concepts of permission, respect, and empowerment in their own sexual interactions and relationships in order to confront these detrimental attitudes and beliefs. To gain the self-assurance and abilities required to honestly express one's wants and desires, this may entail partaking in activities like boundary-setting, assertiveness training, and communication skills. Within the field of erotic wizardry, practitioners can cultivate an atmosphere of empowerment, safety, and respect by confronting negative attitudes and beliefs about power, consent, and boundaries.

This will enable everyone to feel free to freely and authentically explore and express their erotic potential. Furthermore, myths and misconceptions about pleasure, desire, and intimacy are frequently reinforced by societal conditioning surrounding sexuality. People may feel under pressure to live up to unreasonable expectations or ideals in a culture that frequently places a premium on performance and achievement in sexual encounters. This can cause feelings of inadequacy, irritation, or alienation. Similarly, myths and misunderstandings about intimacy, pleasure, and desire may also be perpetuated by societal indoctrination, which can cause emotions of guilt or shame regarding one's sensual experiences and wants. By adopting a more holistic and inclusive understanding of pleasure, desire, and intimacy that respects the varied needs and preferences of each person, practitioners are urged to dispel these myths and prejudices. This could be developing a deeper connection with one's own pleasure and desire as well as the pleasure and desire of others by practising mindfulness, sensory awareness, or erotic exploration. Within the field of erotic wizardry, practitioners can establish a culture of authenticity, vulnerability, and connection by dispelling myths and misconceptions about pleasure, desire, and intimacy.

This will enable everyone to feel free to explore and express their erotic potential in a joyful, authentic, and confident manner. To sum up, overcoming cultural conditioning and the stigma associated with sexuality is a crucial part of the erotic magic path. By acknowledging and confronting the effects of cultural conditioning and stigma, professionals can recover their authority, free themselves from restrictive ideas, and set off on a path of self-exploration, empowerment, and metamorphosis. Adopting these techniques as novices in the field of erotic wizardry can result in deep realizations, healing, and transformation, enabling practitioners to move confidently, honourably, and reverently through the complex terrain of sensual energy.

Building resilience and perseverance in the practice

Practitioners in the enchanted field of erotic wizards frequently go on a path fraught with difficulties, disappointments, and uncertainty. Erotic exploration is not always an easy route, whether it involves traversing societal conditioning, overcoming personal hurdles, or facing outside impediments. But practitioners can overcome these obstacles with elegance, courage, and resolve by developing resilience and tenacity, which will help them realize the full potential of their erotic adventure. Here, we examine the significance of developing fortitude and tenacity in the practice of erotic wizardry and provide methods for nurturing these vital attributes while travelling down the path of inquiry and revelation. Being resilient means having the capacity to adjust and recover from hardships, obstacles, or failures.

Resilience in the context of erotic magic enables practitioners to negotiate the intricacies of their path with power, grace, and adaptability—even when faced with uncertainty or difficulties. Building resilience entails building external supports like community, mentoring, and guidance in addition to interior resources like self-awareness, self-compassion, and self-regulation. In order to gain deeper awareness of their thoughts, feelings, and sensations, as well as to create a sense of calm and inner peace in the face of hardship, practitioners are advised to foster resilience by partaking in practices like mindfulness, meditation, or breathwork.

It is also beneficial for practitioners to look for support from groups and like-minded people who share their goals and ideals, as well as from mentors or teachers who may provide direction and encouragement along the road. By strengthening their resilience, practitioners can face the obstacles on their erotic journey with more grace, assurance, and fortitude, which opens the door to a deeper sense of empowerment, fulfilment, and connection. A person who possesses perseverance is persistent and determined to follow their course despite challenges, setbacks, or difficulties. Perseverance is the quality that enables practitioners of erotic magic to remain dedicated to their path of research and discovery in the face of obstacles or doubts.

Cultivating a feeling of purpose, passion, and dedication to one's mission are all important aspects of building persistence, as are traits like tenacity, patience, and perseverance. By establishing specific objectives and intents for their sexual journey and creating a plan or strategy to reach those objectives, practitioners are urged to develop persistence. Developing a strong support system of friends, family, and also mentors who can provide guidance and encouragement along the road, as well as developing a feeling of purpose and enthusiasm for their journey, can also be beneficial to practitioners. A deeper sense of fulfilment, progress, and transformation can arise when practitioners develop perseverance because it enables them to remain dedicated to their path of study and discovery, even in the face of difficulties or setbacks. Self-care and self-nurturing are strategies that can help develop resilience and tenacity in the practice of erotic wizardry. Self-care is the deliberate action of feeding and nourishing oneself on all levels—physical, emotional, mental, and spiritual—with the goal of fostering increased energy, resilience, and well-being. Exercise, eating a balanced diet, getting restorative sleep, practising relaxation techniques, engaging in creative endeavours, spending time in nature, and asking friends, family, or mentors for help when required are examples of self-care activities.

In addition to recharging their energy stores, practitioners can lessen stress and burnout and develop more resilience and tenacity in their exploration and discovery journeys by making self-care and self-nurturing a priority. The development of awareness and presence is another method for enhancing resiliency and persistence in the practice of erotic magic. By practising mindfulness, individuals can notice their thoughts, feelings, and sensations with compassion and curiosity by bringing non-judgmental awareness to the present moment.

Through practising mindfulness, individuals can become more resilient and persistent by learning how to face obstacles with greater clarity, knowledge, and composure. A few examples of mindfulness activities are body awareness exercises, breathing techniques, and meditation. Other informal mindfulness techniques include mindful eating, walking, and listening. Practitioners can cultivate a deeper sense of serenity, balance, and inner strength by practising mindfulness and present, which can increase their resilience and tenacity in the face of difficulties and uncertainty. Furthermore, developing resilience and endurance in the practice of erotic wizardry necessitates a readiness to accept failure and grow from errors. Failing is an opportunity for learning, development, and self-discovery rather than a sign of weakness or incompetence. It is recommended that practitioners, rather than becoming disheartened or giving up, tackle obstacles and failures with an open mind and a readiness to learn from their experiences. In their quest for knowledge, practitioners can develop greater resilience and perseverance by accepting failure as an unavoidable and natural part of the learning process.

This will enable a deeper feeling of progress, wisdom, and self-awareness to emerge. Finally, in order to navigate the difficulties, disappointments, and uncertainties of the erotic journey with grace, courage, and resolve, developing resilience and perseverance in the practice of erotic wizardry is crucial. A deeper sense of fulfilment, connection, and empowerment can arise when practitioners develop resilience and perseverance through practices like self-care and self-nurturing, mindfulness and presence, and accepting failure as a chance for growth and learning. These practices also help practitioners navigate the complexities of their journey with greater ease, confidence, and resilience. Adopting these techniques can help practitioners who are new to the field of erotic wizardry gain significant insights, healing, and change. This will enable them to move confidently, honourably, and reverently through the complex terrain of erotic energy.

CHAPTER IX

Mastery and Beyond: The Continuing Journey

Reflections on the journey of mastering erotic wizardry

Learning erotic magic is a profoundly transforming path that leads to spiritual growth, empowerment, and self-discovery. Practitioners are asked to explore the depths of their sensual nature, discover the secrets of sexual energy, and awaken the divine in their relationships and themselves as they set out on this journey. Practitioners may face obstacles, disappointments, and times of uncertainty along the road, but with commitment, tenacity, and an open mind, they may successfully negotiate the complex terrain of erotic energy with bravery, grace, and sincerity. Here, we provide our reflections on the way towards mastering erotic magic, along with advice and insights for those who aspire to follow this holy route of inquiry and revelation. Understanding the interdependence of all creatures and the innate divinity in each person is among the most deep insights on the path to becoming an expert in erotic wizardry. Practitioners discover that all life is imbued with the divine essence of love and desire as they gain a deeper awareness of erotic energy and its capacity for change and healing. Practitioners develop a greater feeling of connection, intimacy, and reverence in their relationships by learning to recognize and appreciate the divine inside themselves and their partners through practices including tantra, Taoist sexual development, and sacred sexuality. A greater sense of harmony and togetherness can arise when practitioners approach their path of mastering erotic wizardry with humility, appreciation, and reverence—a recognition of the underlying divinity within themselves and others. Realizing that true mastery is about submitting to the flow of sensual energy and letting it direct and inspire one's actions rather than about control or dominance is another way to reflect on the path of mastering erotic wizardry.

In a society that frequently exalts control and dominance in sexual relationships, practitioners could experience pressure to live up to particular standards or perform, which could result in tension, anxiety, or a sense of being cut off. True mastery of sensual magic, however, requires giving in to the erotic energy's natural flow and letting it direct and inspire one's actions with honesty, grace, and ease. By engaging in techniques like breathwork, sensory awareness, and mindfulness, practitioners can develop a stronger bond with their bodies and desires, which opens up new avenues for the intuitive and spontaneous release of erotic energy. In their sexual experiences and relationships, practitioners can experience a deeper sense of fulfilment, pleasure, and presence when they submit to the flow of erotic energy. This allows for a more unfettered and authentic expression of their erotic nature.

Reflecting on the path to erotic wizardry mastery also involves realizing how crucial self-acceptance and self-awareness are to developing a stronger bond with one's sensual side. Practitioners may discover facets of themselves that they had previously suppressed or rejected as a result of cultural taboos or societal indoctrination as they develop a deeper awareness of who they are and what they want. But real erotic wizardry mastery is accepting and loving every part of oneself, including the dark and the light, the joy and the suffering, with kindness, curiosity, and acceptance. A deeper sense of wholeness, integration, and authenticity can arise when practitioners learn to accept the whole spectrum of their erotic nature through practices like self-inquiry, shadow work, and sensual exploration. In their erotic journey, practitioners can experience a deeper sense of freedom, liberation, and empowerment by developing self-awareness and self-acceptance. This enables a more real and meaningful expression of their dreams and wants.

Furthermore, when one considers the path to erotic magic mastery, one comes to the conclusion that actual mastery is a continuous process of education, development, and progress. Practitioners find that there is always more to learn, more to explore, and more to discover on their path as they gain a deeper awareness of erotic energy and its potential for healing and transformation. The key to mastering erotic magic is to embrace the journey with openness, curiosity, and humility - not to reach a goal or attain a certain degree of expertise, but to embrace the ups and downs, struggles and victories, moments of joy and pain. Practitioners can continue to strengthen their connection with erotic energy and open themselves up to a more profound and transformational experience of love, desire, and intimacy by making a commitment to lifelong learning and self-discovery. Practitioners can enjoy a deeper sense of fulfilment, connection, and empowerment in their erotic journey by embracing the path of mastering erotic wizardry with openness, curiosity, and humility. This allows for a more real and uninhibited expression of their sensual nature.

To sum up, developing erotic wizardry is a profound and life-changing path that leads to empowerment, spiritual development, and self-discovery. A more profound and transforming experience of love, desire, and intimacy can arise via practitioners' deepening of their awareness of erotic energy and its potential for healing and change through practices like sacred sexuality, Taoist sexual cultivation, and tantra. Practitioners can enjoy a deeper sense of fulfilment, connection, and empowerment in their erotic journey by embracing the path of mastering erotic wizardry with openness, curiosity, and humility. This allows for a more real and uninhibited expression of their sensual nature. Accepting these reflections as novices in the field of erotic wizardry can result in deep understanding, healing, and transformation, enabling practitioners to move confidently, honourably, and reverently through the complex terrain of sensual energy.

Suggestions for further exploration and advanced practices

Practitioners may find themselves drawn to investigate increasingly complex methods and tactics as they go deeper into the world of sexual wizardry in order to improve their comprehension and mastery of erotic energy. These cutting-edge techniques open doors to new experiences of fulfilment, empowerment, and connection while also providing chances for deep healing, transformation, and spiritual development.

Here, we provide insights and recommendations for additional research and sophisticated erotic magic techniques, assisting individuals who wish to carry on their quest for knowledge and understanding. The study and synthesis of old mystical traditions and wisdom teachings is one recommendation for additional research and advanced practice in erotic wizardry. As a means of achieving spiritual enlightenment and unity with the divine, societies all over the world have created sacred customs and rituals for respecting and utilizing erotic energy throughout history. Through the study and use of these age-old practices, practitioners can get a greater understanding of the mystical aspects of erotic energy and its capacity for transcendence, healing, and transformation. This could entail studying traditions like Taoist sexual cultivation, Kabbalistic mysticism, Sufi erotic poetry, or tantra; it could also entail practising techniques like energy cultivation exercises, sacred sexuality rituals, or meditation on erotic archetypes. Through the incorporation of archaic mystical customs into their work, practitioners can access timeless knowledge and reach unprecedented profundities and strength in their investigation of sensual energy. The cultivation of ecstatic states of consciousness through breathwork, movement, and sound is another proposal for additional research and advanced practice in erotic wizardry. Ecstatic states of consciousness are reached by activating erotic energy, which allows one to transcend conventional reality and reach higher states of awareness, bliss, and union. A deeper sense of ecstasy, connection, and liberation can arise when practitioners engage in activities like breathwork, dance, or vocalization, which awaken and channel sensual energy throughout their bodies. This can include exploring altered states of consciousness safely and responsibly with psychedelics or plant medicines, as well as engaging in practices like ecstatic dancing, chanting of sacred mantras, or tantric breathing methods. Through the cultivation of ecstatic states of consciousness, practitioners can access an endless source of erotic energy within themselves and feel a stronger sense of unity with the universe and the divine. As a means of achieving more intimacy, trust, and surrender, it is also recommended that conscious kink and BDSM (bondage, discipline, domination, submission, sadism, and masochism) practices be further explored and advanced in erotic wizardry.

In order to promote erotic exploration, healing, and personal development, conscious kink and BDSM practices entail the consensual investigation of power dynamics, role-playing, and sensory experiences. Practitioners can explore and embrace all facets of themselves and their desires through activities like bondage, sensory play, and erotic role-playing. This allows for a deeper sense of authenticity, vulnerability, and empowerment to develop.

To make sure that everyone feels secure, respected, and supported while they explore kink and BDSM relations, this may entail techniques like aftercare, negotiation, and communication. A more genuine and free expression of one's erotic side can be achieved by practitioners who embrace conscious kink and BDSM practices, which help them develop deeper levels of intimacy, trust, and connection with both themselves and their partners. To strengthen the flow of erotic energy and enable deeper levels of healing and transformation, it is also suggested that erotic wizardry be further explored and practised through the integration of bodywork therapies and energy healing.

Working with the body's subtle energy systems, energy healing and bodywork treatments like Reiki, shiatsu, or tantric massage aim to clear blockages, regulate energy flow, and encourage physical, emotional, and spiritual healing. Practitioners can improve the flow of erotic energy throughout their bodies and facilitate a greater sense of pleasure, relaxation, and connection by combining energy healing and bodywork into their practices. To release tension, open, energetic channels, and develop increased sensitivity and awareness to erotic energy, this may entail techniques like self-massage, partner massage, or energy healing sessions with a qualified practitioner.

Practitioners can enhance their relationship with erotic energy and feel a greater sense of fullness, vigour, and well-being in their erotic journey by incorporating bodywork and energy healing therapies into their practice. Finally, recommendations for additional research and sophisticated erotic magic techniques present practitioners with chances for deep metamorphosis, recovery, and spiritual development. Practitioners can tap into new levels of empowerment, pleasure, and connection in their exploration of erotic energy by studying and incorporating ancient mystical traditions, exploring conscious kink and BDSM practices, cultivating ecstatic states of consciousness, and incorporating energy healing and bodywork modalities into their practice. A greater sense of fulfilment, connection, and release can arise when practitioners embrace these concepts with openness, curiosity, and humility as they proceed on their journey of research and discovery. Embracing these recommendations can help practitioners negotiate the complex terrain of erotic energy with confidence, integrity, and reverence. For those who are new to the field of erotic magic, it can result in remarkable discoveries, healing, and transformation.

Encouragement to continue evolving and deepening one's magical practice

Practitioners are called to engage on a road of continuous expansion, growth, and strengthening of their magical practice in the sacred journey of mastering sexual wizardry.

Erotic exploration is a process of continuous self-discovery, empowerment, and transformation rather than a final destination. A greater connection with oneself, one's partners, and the divine can arise when practitioners accept the trip with openness, curiosity, and humility as they negotiate the complex terrain of erotic energy. Here, we provide support for continuing to develop and enhance one's magical practice, as well as wisdom and direction for anyone wishing to follow this holy route of inquiry and learning. Realizing that erotic energy has the limitless capacity to heal, transform, and awaken the soul is one of the most powerful motivators to keep developing and honing one's magical craft. Strong and pervasive, erotic energy permeates every part of life, from the most ordinary to the most sublime. Through the process of acknowledging and utilizing erotic energy as a means of achieving spiritual enlightenment and merging with the divine, practitioners can experience unprecedented levels of fulfilment, empowerment, and joy in their lives. Practitioners find that there is always more to learn, more to explore, and more to discover on their path as they gain a deeper awareness of erotic energy and its potential for healing and transformation.

The key to mastering erotic magic is to embrace the journey with openness, curiosity, and humility - not to reach a goal or attain a certain degree of expertise, but to embrace the ups and downs, struggles and victories, moments of joy and pain. Practitioners can enjoy a deeper sense of fulfilment, connection, and empowerment in their erotic journey by embracing the path of mastering erotic wizardry with openness, curiosity, and humility.

This allows for a more real and uninhibited expression of their sensual nature. Realizing the interdependence of all beings and the innate divinity in each person is another motivation to keep developing and strengthening one's magical practice. Practitioners discover that all life is imbued with the divine essence of love and desire as they gain a deeper awareness of erotic energy and its capacity for change and healing. Practitioners develop a greater feeling of connection, intimacy, and reverence in their relationships by learning to recognize and appreciate the divine inside themselves and their partners through practices including tantra, Taoist sexual development, and sacred sexuality. A greater sense of harmony and togetherness can arise when practitioners approach their path of mastering erotic wizardry with humility, appreciation, and reverence—a recognition of the underlying divinity within themselves and others. Furthermore, acknowledging the significance of self-acceptance and self-awareness in developing a stronger bond with one's sensual side is a call to keep developing and strengthening one's magical practice. Practitioners may discover facets of themselves that they had previously suppressed or rejected as a result of cultural taboos or societal indoctrination as they develop a deeper awareness of who they are and what they want.

But real erotic wizardry mastery is accepting and loving every part of oneself, including the dark and the light, the joy and the suffering, with kindness, curiosity, and acceptance. A deeper sense of wholeness, integration, and authenticity can arise when practitioners learn to accept the whole spectrum of their erotic nature through practices like self-inquiry, shadow work, and sensual exploration. In their erotic journey, practitioners can experience a deeper sense of freedom, liberation, and empowerment by developing self-awareness and self-acceptance. This enables a more real and meaningful expression of their dreams and wants. Recognizing the value of mentorship and community in offering support, direction, and inspiration along the way is another way to be inspired to keep developing and strengthening one's magical practice. Mentors offer knowledge, direction, and encouragement to help practitioners overcome their limitations and realize their full potential, while communities offer a sense of validation, support, and belonging that may be extremely helpful in navigating the difficulties and uncertainties of the sexual journey. It is recommended that practitioners look for communities and persons who share their beliefs and goals, as well as mentors or teachers who have been there before and can provide advice and support along the journey. On their path to erotic wizardry, practitioners can develop the bravery, fortitude, and perseverance necessary to go beyond roadblocks and hurdles by surrounding themselves with a supportive group and asking mentors for advice.

Conclusively, the route towards mastering erotic wizardry is a sacred one that involves investigation, transformation, and discovery. Through an open, curious, and humble embrace of the journey, practitioners can experience unprecedented levels of fulfilment, empowerment, and connection in their lives. The unlimited potential of erotic energy, the connectivity of all creatures, the significance of self-awareness and self-acceptance, and the value of community and mentorship are all invited to be embraced by practitioners as they continue their journey of exploration and also discovery. In their erotic journey, practitioners can feel a greater feeling of fulfilment, connection, and empowerment by developing and deepening their magical practices. This enables a more genuine and free expression of their erotic nature. Accepting these suggestions as novices in the field of erotic wizardry can result in deep realizations, healing, and transformation, enabling practitioners to move confidently, honourably, and reverently through the complex terrain of sensual energy.

CHAPTER X

The Power of Erotic Expression

Exploring the role of self-expression in unlocking erotic potential

The investigation of self-expression as a way to unleash the full potential of sensual energy is one of the most profound and transformational components of the journey toward mastering erotic wizardry. Self-expression allows practitioners to access the depths of their erotic nature and build a deeper sense of pleasure, connection, and empowerment. It entails expressing one's wants, fantasies, and feelings in a variety of original and genuine ways. Here, we examine how self-expression can be used to unlock one's erotic potential and offer advice and insights to those who wish to go off on this holy path of self-discovery. Self-expression is essential to releasing one's erotic potential because it gives people a way to assertively and honestly express their wants, boundaries, and desires. Many people may find it difficult to communicate who they really are and to stand up for their needs in relationships and sexual encounters because they live in a society that frequently discourages honest and open dialogue about sex and desire.

On the other hand, practitioners can recover their agency and voice in matters of sexuality by accepting self-expression as a means of empowerment. This opens the door to a more profound sense of closeness, authenticity, and fulfilment. In addition to having open and honest conversations with partners about preferences, boundaries, and permission, this may entail engaging in activities like journaling, role-playing, or creative writing to explore and articulate one's desires, fantasies, and boundaries. In their romantic encounters and relationships, practitioners can foster a culture of empowerment, respect, and mutual understanding by embracing self-expression as a means of communicating openly and assertively. This will make the experience of sensual energy more gratifying and enriching. Additionally, self-expression is essential to releasing one's erotic potential since it gives people the freedom, curiosity, and inventiveness to embrace and explore many facets of their sensual nature. A complex and dynamic force, erotic energy embraces a broad spectrum of fantasies, wants, and emotions, from the sensual and romantic to the outrageous and forbidden. Practitioners can access the depths of their fantasies, feelings, and desires by accepting self-expression as a way to explore and embrace the complete spectrum of erotic energy. This enables a deeper sense of fulfilment, pleasure, and excitement to arise. This can entail engaging in role-playing, fantasy exploration, or sexual experimentation to broaden one's sensual repertoire and find new sources of pleasure and arousal, as well as activities like erotic art, dance, or performance to explore and express many elements of one's erotic self. Professionals can develop a deeper sense of self-awareness, self-acceptance, and self-love by embracing self-expression as a way to explore and appreciate the complete spectrum of erotic energy. This enables a more honest and unfettered expression of their erotic nature.

Furthermore, self-expression helps people embrace their actual selves with courage, confidence, and authenticity by giving them a way to let go of their inhibitions, shame, and fear related to their sexuality. This helps people reach their full sensual potential. Many people may find it difficult to fully and truly embrace their erotic nature in a society that frequently stigmatizes and shames sexual desire, which can result in emotions of guilt, embarrassment, or inadequacy. But by accepting self-expression as a means of achieving liberation, practitioners can cast off the chains of guilt and anxiety and bravely, authentically, and confidently embrace who they really are. To appreciate and honour one's body, wants, and experiences may entail engaging in activities like erotic embodiment exercises, body-positive affirmations, or sexual storytelling. It may also entail advocating for change in the community by challenging prevailing ideas and norms regarding sexuality. Practitioners can develop a greater feeling of self-acceptance, empowerment, and liberation by embracing self-expression as a way to let go of inhibitions, shame, and fear. This makes it possible to experience sensual energy in a more happy, delightful, and nourishing way. To sum up, self-expression is essential to releasing one's erotic potential since it allows people to express themselves freely, communicate honestly, and overcome feelings of guilt and anxiety related to their sexuality. A greater sense of authenticity, intimacy, and fulfilment can arise when practitioners regain their voice and agency in matters of eroticism by embracing self-expression as a means of empowerment. For those who are new to the world of erotic magic, accepting self-expression can result in life-changing experiences, healing, and profound revelations.

This will enable practitioners to move confidently, honourably, and reverently over the complex terrain of sensual energy. Through the process of self-expression, practitioners can access the depths of their fantasies, emotions, and desires, enabling a more unfettered and true expression of their sexual nature. This allows practitioners to explore and accept the complete spectrum of erotic energy.

Techniques for embracing and communicating desires authentically

A key component of the path of sexual wizardry is embracing and expressing desires in a true way. This enables practitioners to access the whole potential of their erotic nature and develop greater degrees of closeness, fulfilment, and connection in their relationships. Honouring and respecting the aspirations of others while being open and honest in expressing one's own wants, needs, and boundaries is a key component of authentic desire communication. In order to help practitioners who want to improve their capacity to communicate their erotic impulses with integrity, clarity, and sincerity, we examine a variety of methods and approaches for accepting and expressing desires in this section. A vital method for accepting and expressing wishes in a genuine manner is to engage in self-awareness and self-reflection exercises. It is crucial for practitioners to investigate and comprehend their own desires, preferences, and boundaries before communicating them to a partner. This is exploring the deeper levels of one's sensual nature through introspection, reflection, and self-inquiry. Journaling, mindfulness exercises, and meditation can help practitioners become more self-aware and clear about their aspirations. A deeper degree of connection and intimacy can arise when practitioners articulate their desires to their partners with greater authenticity, confidence, and clarity, all thanks to a deeper awareness of their own wishes. Using active listening and empathy is another method for embracing and expressing wants in a genuine way.

In order to be truly authentic, one must listen intently and sympathetically to the desires of others in addition to expressing one's own. It is recommended that practitioners listen to their partner's desires without passing judgment or interjecting; instead, they should approach communication with an open mind and heart.

In order to establish a more profound feeling of trust, understanding, and connection in their relationships, practitioners who engage in active listening and empathy exercises can provide a secure and encouraging environment in which their partners can freely and honestly communicate their goals. Practitioners can also thank and appreciate their partner for being open and vulnerable by validating and acknowledging their wants. Practitioners can develop deeper levels of closeness and connection in their relationships by engaging in active listening and empathy exercises. This enables both parties to have more rewarding and gratifying sensual experiences. Moreover, using straightforward language is a strategy for accepting and expressing wants in an authentic way. Genuine communication entails articulating goals in an unambiguous way and using language that is sincere, courteous, and judgment-free. Practitioners are advised to express their desires clearly and precisely rather than using unclear or imprecise terminology. This could entail making use of "I" phrases to convey individual preferences and wishes, like "I feel most connected when we..." or "I would love it if we could try..." Practitioners can minimize misunderstandings and miscommunications by communicating with their partners in a straightforward and concise manner, which guarantees that their wishes are acknowledged and understood. Practitioners are also urged to invite their partners to communicate their own preferences and wishes in an atmosphere of mutual inquiry and understanding and to be receptive to criticism and conversation.

Moreover, practising vulnerability and courage is a method for accepting and expressing wishes in a genuine way. In order to engage in authentic communication, practitioners must be brave and willing to show vulnerability while sharing their desires in an honest and open manner, even when they are unsure or afraid of being rejected. This could entail voicing wishes that might be viewed as unusual or taboo and moving outside of one's comfort zone. It is recommended that practitioners approach communication with an open heart and a desire to be recognized and welcomed for their true selves. In order to facilitate a more genuine and satisfying expression of their fantasies and needs, practitioners can build stronger intimacy and connections in their relationships by embracing vulnerability and courage. Additionally, the art of compromise and negotiation is a method for embracing and expressing aspirations in a genuine way. In order to reach mutually acceptable agreements, genuine communication entails not only articulating demands but also being prepared to bargain and compromise with partners. It is recommended that practitioners approach communication with an attitude of cooperation and collaboration, looking for points of agreement that respect the interests and preferences of both parties.

This could entail talking about limits, looking into novel options, and coming up with original solutions that satisfy the requirements of both parties. In order to create a more satisfying and harmonious sensual experience for both parties, practitioners can cultivate a greater feeling of trust, respect, and understanding in their relationships by engaging in negotiation and compromise exercises. To sum up, a key component of the path of erotic wizardry is the honest acceptance and communication of wants. This enables practitioners to access the full potential of their erotic nature and develop greater degrees of closeness, fulfilment, and connection in their relationships. A deeper sense of intimacy and connection with oneself and one's partners can be fostered by practitioners honing their skills in self-awareness and self-reflection, active listening and empathy, clear and direct language, vulnerability and courage, negotiation and compromise, and vulnerability and courage.

Embracing these approaches as novices in the field of erotic wizardry can result in significant revelations, healing, and transformation, enabling practitioners to move confidently, honourably, and reverently through the complex terrain of sensual energy.

Exercises for cultivating confidence and self- assurance in erotic expression

As they explore and truly express their desires, fantasies, and boundaries, practitioners of erotic wizardry must develop a strong sense of confidence and self-assurance. The path of erotic expression can occasionally be difficult because people may find it difficult to completely embrace their erotic nature due to cultural standards and personal fears.

However, practitioners can develop self-assurance and confidence in their erotic expression by deliberate practice and investigation, which opens the door to a greater sense of fulfilment, empowerment, and authenticity in their interactions with others and in their experiences. This section delves into a variety of exercises and methods that help practitioners develop clarity, conviction, and integrity in their erotic expression. It also offers insights and recommendations for those who want to improve their communication skills. The practice of positive self-talk and self-affirmations is a useful tool for developing self-assurance and confidence in sensual expression. Consciously stating positive things about oneself, such as "I am worthy of love and pleasure" or "I trust myself to express my desires authentically," is known as self-affirmation. Through consistent repetition of these affirmations, practitioners can rewire their subconscious mind to accept their intrinsic value and their capacity for self-expression that is both assured and genuine. Positive self-talk also entails changing self-limiting or negative thoughts to ones that are empowering and encouraging.

To reframe the statement "I'm not good enough," for instance, practitioners can say something like "I am enough just as I am, and I have the courage to express myself authentically." Practitioners can develop a stronger sense of confidence and self-assurance in their erotic expression by engaging in self-affirmation and positive self-talk practices. This will enable a more empowered and free experience of their fantasies and desires. The practice of embodiment and sensory awareness is another exercise that helps develop self-assurance and confidence in erotic expression. In order to express desires and pleasures in a more embodied and genuine way, embodiment entails developing a close relationship with one's body and senses. To develop more bodily awareness and presence, practitioners can try techniques like sensuous movement, body scanning, and mindful breathing. Practitioners can become more confident and authentic in their expression of their erotic nature by learning to trust their body's wisdom and intuition by tuning into the sensations of pleasure and desire that develop inside the body. Furthermore, practitioners can improve their ability to express themselves sensually and strengthen their relationship with their sensual selves by experimenting with many senses, including taste, smell, touch, and sound. A more satisfying and rewarding erotic experience can be had by practitioners who practice embodiment and sensual awareness because it helps them develop a stronger feeling of self-assurance and confidence in their capacity to express themselves truthfully and sensually. Moreover, practising assertiveness and setting boundaries is a good way to develop confidence and self-assurance in sensual expression. In order to preserve a feeling of safety, respect, and autonomy during erotic relationships, practitioners need to feel strong and capable enough to express their boundaries. By considering their own needs, wants, and boundaries and expressing them to their partners in an aggressive and straightforward manner, practitioners can practice creating boundaries.

This could entail expressing limits with "I" phrases, like "I need..." or "I feel uncomfortable when..." Before progressively moving up to more personal contacts, practitioners are advised to practice setting boundaries in low-stakes scenarios first, such as with friends or in non-erotic environments. Through the practice of assertiveness and boundary-setting, individuals can develop a stronger feeling of self-assurance and confidence in their capacity to communicate their needs and boundaries in an authentic manner, which can lead to a deeper level of intimacy, respect, and trust in their relationships. Moreover, practising vulnerability and bravery is a good way to develop confidence and self-assurance in erotic expression. In order to engage in authentic erotic expression, practitioners must be brave and willing to share their thoughts and desires in an honest and open manner, even when they are uncertain or afraid of being rejected. Vulnerability practitioners enable themselves to be seen and accepted for who they really are by confiding in trusted friends or lovers about their thoughts and aspirations in a secure and encouraging setting. Practitioners can also demonstrate courage by venturing outside of their comfort zone and taking chances when expressing wishes that can be seen as unusual or taboo. Practitioners can gain a greater sense of confidence and assurance in their ability to express themselves honestly and boldly by accepting their vulnerability and bravery. This can result in a more liberating and powerful experience of their erotic nature.

Moreover, practising manifestation and visualization is a good way to develop self-assurance and confidence in sensual expression.

Through vivid mental rehearsal of desired events and outcomes, visualization helps practitioners embody the sensations of fulfilment, empowerment, and confidence that go along with their objectives. Practitioners can picture themselves voicing their wants with assurance and sincerity, imagining the sensation in their bodies and the good reactions of their partners to their communication. In addition, practitioners can engage in manifestation by focusing on their desired sensual experiences and making affirmations for them, believing that the cosmos will assist them in realizing their goals. A more rewarding and gratifying erotic journey can be had by practitioners who regularly practice visualization and manifestation because it helps them develop a stronger sense of confidence and self-assurance in their abilities to express their desires authentically and create their ideal sensual experiences.

To sum up, developing self-assurance and confidence in sensual expression is an essential part of the erotic magic path. It enables practitioners to access the full potential of their erotic nature and express themselves bravely and genuinely. Practitioners can improve their capacity to express their desires with clarity, conviction, and integrity, fostering a deeper sense of authenticity, empowerment, and fulfilment in their relationships and experiences. These practices include practising self-affirmations and positive self-talk, embodiment and sensual awareness, boundary-setting and assertiveness, vulnerability and courage, and visualization and manifestation. Embracing these techniques as novices in the field of erotic wizardry can result in deep insights, healing, and transformation, enabling practitioners to move confidently, honourably, and reverently through the complex terrain of sensual energy.

CHAPTER XI

Sensory Sorcery Heightening Pleasure Through the Senses

Understanding the importance of sensory experiences in eroticism

In the world of sexuality, sensory encounters are essential because they open doors to increased pleasure, closeness, and connection. The five senses—taste, smell, sight, touch, and sound—are potent tools that people use to interact with and interpret their surroundings. When used purposefully, they may also add complexity and richness to sensual encounters.

We explore how each sense contributes to the arousal and fulfilment of erotic desires in this section, delving into the significance of sensory experiences in eroticism and offering insights into how practitioners of erotic wizardry can use sensory experiences to cultivate deeper levels of pleasure, intimacy, and connection in their erotic journey. One of the main senses, sight, is important for eroticism because it enables people to recognize and value the physical attractiveness of both themselves and their relationships. Sensual lighting, alluring clothing, and erotic imagery are examples of visual stimuli that can heighten arousal and desire and cause a visceral reaction in the viewer.

Furthermore, the expression of intimacy, passion, and desire through body language and eye contact can fortify the relationship between lovers and enhance the physical experience. By adding visual stimulation to their romantic encounters—whether by the creation of an aesthetically pleasing atmosphere, erotic dance or striptease, or the exploration of erotic photography or art —practitioners of erotic wizardry can effectively harness the power of sight. Through deliberate use of the sense of sight, practitioners can develop a more visually stimulating and rich sensual experience, increase desire, and deepen closeness. Another important sense of eroticism is touch, which provides a direct route to intimacy and physical pleasure. Touch, in all its forms— firm embraces, tender caresses, or playful strokes—can arouse strong feelings of pleasure and arousal, stimulating the senses and intensifying the sensual experience.

Through touch, people can learn more about their partners' and their own body contours, resulting in a stronger sense of closeness and connection. In order to increase arousal and pleasure, practitioners of erotic wizardry might harness the power of touch by experimenting with various tactile sensations, such as soft textiles, textured surfaces, or different pressure levels. Furthermore, adding massage, bodywork, or sensual touch techniques can enhance intimacy and relaxation, making the erotic experience deeper and more satisfying. Practitioners can improve their capacity to connect physically and emotionally with themselves and their partners, leading to deeper degrees of pleasure, closeness, and connection in their sensual encounters, by developing a greater awareness of and appreciation for the sensation of touch. Another important factor in eroticism is taste, which enhances the sensual experience by providing a layer of richness and decadence. Sharing food or beverages with a significant other can be a very sensual and intimate experience that engages the senses of taste and stimulates the senses in novel and exciting ways. Adding aphrodisiac items to your diet or indulging in rich desserts can also increase arousal and pleasure by teasing your taste buds and opening your senses to new sensual possibilities.

Through experimenting with various flavours, textures, and gastronomic delights during their romantic experiences, practitioners of erotic wizardry can harness the power of taste. Through the sensual delights of kissing and licking or indulging in a sensual feast of fruits, chocolates, and wine, practitioners can use taste as a gateway to a deeper level of intimacy and connection with their partners. Experts can develop a deeper understanding of the sensual pleasures of the body and produce more meaningful and gratifying sexual experiences by embracing the sense of taste as a tool for boosting erotic pleasure and connection. Additionally, scent has a strong influence on eroticism, using its ability to evoke memories, feelings, and wants. Some scents can elicit strong sensations of arousal and attraction, intensifying the sensual experience and strengthening the bond between couples. Examples of these scents include pheromones, perfumes, and natural body odours. Aromatherapy and fragrant oils can also increase desire, promote relaxation, and create a sensual, intimate atmosphere during romantic meetings. Erotic wizards might use their sense of smell to their advantage by experimenting with various smells and aromas that speak to their inclinations and desires. Practitioners can create a welcoming and seductive environment that stimulates the sense of smell and heightens the erotic experience, whether they want to use perfumes, scented candles, or essential oils.

Through the use of scent as a tool to increase arousal and intimacy, practitioners can strengthen their bonds with their partners and themselves and produce more pleasant and memorable sensual experiences. Last but not least, sound can be used as a potent technique to heighten erotica by giving it more depth, rhythm, and intensity. Moans, whispers, and sighs are examples of noises that can express closeness, pleasure, and desire. Together, these sounds create a rich aural environment that heightens arousal and strengthens bonds between couples. Incorporating ambient sounds, music, or erotic poetry into romantic interactions can also heighten the mood, increase arousal, and produce a sensual and passionate feeling. Erotic wizards can use sound to their advantage by experimenting with various audio stimuli that speak to their inclinations and desires. It is possible for practitioners to create a multi-layered, intense erotic experience that arouses the senses and deepens the link between them and their partners through the use of sensual music, sexual narrative, and ambient noises like rain or ocean waves. Practitioners can develop a higher understanding and respect for the auditory parts of the sexual experience and create more immersive and rewarding interactions by embracing the sense of sound as a tool for boosting sensual pleasure and connection.

To sum up, sensory experiences are essential to eroticism since they open doors to increased pleasure, closeness, and connection. Sight, touch, taste, smell, sound, and other senses all add to the complexity and richness of the sensual experience, giving practitioners intriguing new avenues to explore and express their desires. An erotic trip can be made more rewarding and satisfying for practitioners of erotic wizardry by cultivating deeper levels of pleasure, intimacy, and connection in their relationships and experiences through the use of sensory sensations. Accepting the significance of sensory experiences as novices in the field of erotic wizardry can result in deep realizations, healing, and transformation, enabling practitioners to move confidently, honourably, and reverently through the complex terrain of erotic energy.

Utilizing sensory stimulation to enhance intimacy and pleasure

Intimacy and pleasure are greatly increased during romantic meetings when there is sensory stimulation present. This provides erotic wizards with a wide range of feelings to experience and appreciate. Through deliberate activation of the five senses—taste, smell, taste, touch, and sound—people can enhance their intimacy with one another and themselves, resulting in more satisfying and immersive sensual encounters. We explore how each sense contributes to the arousal and satisfaction of erotic desires in this section, delving into the art of using sensory stimulation to enhance intimacy and pleasure. We also offer insights into how practitioners can integrate sensory techniques into their erotic encounters to cultivate deeper levels of fulfilment, pleasure, and connection.

One of the most effective senses to use to heighten intimacy and pleasure in intimate relationships is sight. Setting the atmosphere for a more immersive and fulfilling experience, visual cues like sensual lighting, alluring clothing, and sexy artwork can evoke desire and fuel passion. In order to enhance the mood and atmosphere of their interactions, practitioners of erotic wizardry might harness the power of sight by creating an environment that is visually exciting and combining components like sumptuous textiles, enticing artwork, and gentle candlelight. In order to strengthen their bond and arousal through the act of seeing and being seen, practitioners can also delve into the practice of sensual observation, which involves taking the time to notice and value the physical attractiveness of both themselves and their partners. Practitioners can generate more visually rich and stimulating experiences with sex, leading to a deeper sense of fulfilment and connection with their partners by embracing the sense of sight as a tool for boosting intimacy and pleasure. Another crucial component of sensory stimulation for boosting intimacy and enjoyment in intimate experiences is touch. Touch, in all its forms—firm embraces, tender caresses, or playful strokes—can produce strong feelings of pleasure and arousal, strengthening the bond between lovers and intensifying the sensual experience. To increase arousal and pleasure, practitioners of erotic wizardry might use touch to their advantage by experimenting with various tactile sensations, such as silk sheets, textured textiles, or different pressure levels.

Furthermore, adding massage, bodywork, or sensual touch techniques can enhance intimacy and relaxation, making the erotic experience deeper and more satisfying. Practitioners can improve their capacity to connect physically and emotionally with themselves and their partners, leading to deeper degrees of pleasure, closeness, and connection in their sensual encounters, by developing a greater awareness of and appreciation for the sensation of touch. Intimacy and pleasure during intimate encounters are also greatly enhanced by taste, which adds a level of sensory richness and indulgence to the experience. Sharing food or beverages with a significant other can be a very sensual and intimate experience that engages the senses of taste and stimulates the senses in novel and exciting ways. Adding aphrodisiac items to your diet or indulging in rich desserts can also increase arousal and pleasure by teasing your taste buds and opening your senses to new sensual possibilities.

Through experimenting with various flavours, textures, and gastronomic delights during their romantic experiences, practitioners of erotic wizardry can harness the power of taste. Through the sensual delights of kissing and licking or indulging in a sensual feast of fruits, chocolates, and wine, practitioners can use taste as a gateway to a deeper level of intimacy and connection with their partners. Experts can develop a deeper understanding of the sensual pleasures of the body and produce more meaningful and gratifying sexual experiences by embracing the sense of taste as a tool for boosting erotic pleasure and connection. Additionally, scent has a powerful ability to evoke memories, emotions, and wants, which enhances intimacy and pleasure during intimate experiences. Some scents can elicit strong sensations of arousal and attraction, intensifying the sensual experience and strengthening the bond between couples. Examples of these scents include pheromones, perfumes, and natural body odours. Aromatherapy and fragrant oils can also increase desire, promote relaxation, and create a sensual, intimate atmosphere during romantic meetings. Erotic wizards might use their sense of smell to their advantage by experimenting with various smells and aromas that speak to their inclinations and desires. Practitioners can create a welcoming and seductive environment that stimulates the sense of smell and heightens the erotic experience, whether they want to use perfumes, scented candles, or essential oils. Through the use of scent as a tool to increase arousal and intimacy, practitioners can strengthen their bonds with their partners and themselves and produce more pleasant and memorable sensual experiences. Last but not least, sound may add depth, rhythm, and intensity to an intimate connection, increasing closeness and enjoyment. Moans, whispers, and sighs are examples of noises that can express closeness, pleasure, and desire.

Together, these sounds create a rich aural environment that heightens arousal and strengthens bonds between couples. Incorporating ambient sounds, music, or erotic poetry into romantic interactions can also heighten the mood, increase arousal, and produce a sensual and passionate feeling. Erotic wizards can use sound to their advantage by experimenting with various audio stimuli that speak to their inclinations and desires. Through the use of sensuous music, sexual narrative, or ambient sounds like rain and ocean waves, practitioners can create a multi-layered, immersive erotic experience that stimulates the senses and strengthens the bond between them and their partners.

Practical exercises for awakening and exploring the senses in lovemaking

Lovemaking is a transforming technique that heightens pleasure, deepens intimacy, and creates a deeper connection between partners by awakening and exploring the senses. Erotic wizards can create more satisfying and immersive erotic experiences by deliberately appealing to the senses, which enables them to enjoy the entire range of sensory delights at their disposal. This section offers insights and assistance for practitioners who wish to improve their sensual awareness and strengthen their connection with their partners. We explore various exercises that can be used to awaken and explore the senses in lovemaking. Sensory deprivation is a useful technique for arousing the senses during romantic interactions.

To increase the sensitivity and awareness of the remaining senses, one or more senses can be temporarily restricted or removed, a practice known as sensory deprivation. In order to investigate sensory deprivation, practitioners can blindfold themselves or their partners, experiment with limiting movement using shackles, or use earphones to block out sound. By restricting the senses in this way, practitioners are able to raise their level of expectation and excitement, which enables them to concentrate more fully on the experiences and feelings of taste, smell, touch, and sound. Couples who go through a period of sensory loss may also grow in their ability to trust and submit as they relinquish control and follow their heightened sensory awareness. Sensory inquiry is another useful activity for investigating the senses in romantic relationships. In order to enhance the feeling of closeness and enjoyment, sensory exploration entails deliberately using each of the senses—sight, touch, taste, smell, and sound. By taking turns blindfolding one another and using different stimuli—such as feathers, silk scarves, fragrant oils, or flavoured lubricants—to arouse the senses, practitioners can investigate sensory exploration. Practitioners can find new sources of pleasure and arousal by concentrating on each sense separately.

This helps them develop a greater understanding and appreciation for the subtleties of feeling. Couples that engage in sensory exploration of each other's bodies and experiences may also develop a stronger sense of closeness and connection. Furthermore, practising attentive contact is a way to stimulate the senses during a romantic encounter. By approaching contact with presence, intention, and awareness, mindful touch enables practitioners to completely lose themselves in the feelings and sensations of touch. By exploring one other's bodies with their hands and paying great attention to the texture, pressure, and temperature of their touches, practitioners can engage in mindful contact. Lovemaking may be made more intimate and satisfying for practitioners by slowing down and appreciating every moment of touch. This helps practitioners connect deeper with both themselves and their partners. In addition, mindful touch can assist practitioners in letting go of tension, worry, and anxiety. This helps people to become more fully present in the moment and enjoy their sensual interactions to the fullest. Additionally, sensual massage is a discipline that explores the senses in the context of lovemaking. In order to stimulate and relax the body and provide a greater level of pleasure and connection, sensual massage uses contact. By using long, deliberate strokes to stimulate the senses and raise desire, practitioners can experiment with sensual massage by alternately stroking each other's bodies with scented oils or lotions.

Through an emphasis on the tactile experience and the transfer of energy between partners, practitioners can enhance their closeness and connection, resulting in a more meaningful and satisfying lovemaking experience. In addition to helping the body release tension and stress, sensual massage helps practitioners become more totally relaxed and enjoy and satisfy their erotic interactions to the fullest. Sensory storytelling is another activity that helps to stimulate the senses during the lovemaking process. The goal of sensory storytelling is to provide both parties with a rich sensory experience by appealing to their senses through language and pictures. Using sensory language to evoke the sights, sounds, smells, tastes, and sensations of their romantic encounters, practitioners can engage in sensory storytelling by taking turns vividly recounting their fantasies, desires, and experiences. Lovemaking can become more intense and satisfying for practitioners when they use their imagination and senses to stimulate deeper connections with both themselves and their partners. In the bedroom, sensory storytelling can also encourage creativity and exploration, enabling lovers to find new sources of arousal and pleasure together.

Finally, practical exercises for arousing and investigating the senses in lovemaking provide practitioners of erotic wizardry with a potent way to enhance pleasure, heighten intimacy, and cultivate a connection with both themselves and their partners. Through techniques such as sensory deprivation, sensory exploration, attentive touch, sensual massage, and sensory storytelling, practitioners can develop an enhanced awareness and appreciation for the sensory delights at their disposal, hence facilitating a more fulfilling and immersive lovemaking experience.

Embracing these hands-on activities can help practitioners gain significant insights, heal, and transform as novices in the field of sexual wizardry. This will enable them to navigate the complex terrain of erotic energy with confidence, integrity, and reverence.

CHAPTER XII

The Alchemy of Connection Deepening Intimacy

Techniques for fostering emotional intimacy and connection in relationships

Relationships that are rewarding and enriching require emotional intimacy and connection because it is the foundation for trust, vulnerability, and love to flourish. In the world of erotic magic, developing emotional closeness and intimacy is crucial to strengthening the tie between lovers and fostering an environment that is safe and nurturing for experimentation and development. This section delves into different methods and approaches that promote emotional closeness and bonding in partnerships. It offers advice and understanding to professionals who wish to fortify the emotional basis of their relationships and improve their erotic exploration and discovery process.

The practice of open and honest communication is one effective way to promote emotional intimacy and connection in partnerships. Healthy and satisfying relationships are built on communication, which enables partners to freely and honestly communicate their needs, wants, and thoughts. By establishing a secure and encouraging environment for candid conversation where both parties feel heard, understood, and appreciated, practitioners of erotic wizardry can foster emotional intimacy and connection. This could entail scheduling specific time for in-depth talks, actively listening to one another without passing judgment or interjecting, and demonstrating compassion and understanding for one another's viewpoints and experiences. Practitioners can increase their emotional connection and establish a solid foundation of intimacy and trust in their relationship by encouraging candid and open conversation. Practising openness and authenticity in relationships is another way to build emotional closeness and connection. Being open and forthcoming with a trustworthy partner about one's worries, insecurities, and weaknesses is a necessary component of vulnerability.

Conversely, authenticity is speaking the truth and being sincere while expressing one's feelings, ideas, and desires. By embracing vulnerability and authenticity in their relationships and allowing themselves to be seen and welcomed for who they truly are, practitioners of erotic wizardry can create emotional closeness and connection. This could entail being present and mindful of one another's wants and desires, as well as exchanging personal thoughts and feelings. Practitioners can strengthen their emotional bond and establish a deeper feeling of intimacy and closeness in their relationships by encouraging openness and authenticity. Moreover, practising empathy and compassion is a strategy for encouraging emotional closeness and connection in relationships. While compassion is the desire to lessen suffering and offer assistance and consolation to those in need, empathy is the capacity to comprehend and share the thoughts, feelings, and experiences of another person. Erotic wizards can develop emotional intimacy and connection by showing empathy and compassion for their partners, as well as by showing them understanding, acceptance, and support at happy, sad, or difficult moments. This can entail paying attention to what the other is saying, encouraging and reassuring each other, and, if necessary, showing physical care and comfort.

Through cultivating empathy and compassion, practitioners can enhance their emotional bond and fortify the love and trust that underpin their partnership. Shared experiences and rituals are another method for promoting emotional closeness and connection in relationships. Partners can improve their relationship, generate enduring memories, and deepen their bond via shared events and rituals. Erotic wizards can foster emotional closeness and connection by participating in rituals and shared activities that are meaningful and personal to both parties. This could include going on romantic dates, taking trips together, commemorating milestones, or establishing customs and rituals that stand in for their dedication to one another. Through exchanging experiences and customs, practitioners can establish a feeling of unity and belonging in their relationship, which strengthens the bond between them on an emotional level as well as their sense of partnership and companionship.

Additionally, practicing mindfulness and present in relationships is a strategy for building emotional closeness and connection. Being totally present and involved in the moment is a technique that encompasses mindfulness and enables practitioners to develop awareness, acceptance, and appreciation for both themselves and their partners. Experts in sensual wizardry can foster emotional closeness and connection by exercising mindfulness in their partnerships, giving each other's needs, wants, and experiences their whole attention. This could entail putting electronics and other distractions away, taking part in peaceful and nourishing pursuits like yoga, meditation, or nature walks, and cherishing intimate and bonding moments. Practitioners can strengthen their emotional bond and establish a deeper sense of intimacy and closeness in their relationship by cultivating mindfulness and presence.

Finally, strategies for building emotional closeness and connection in partnerships provide erotic wizards with a road map for strengthening partner bonds and establishing a safe haven for learning and development. Practitioners can fortify the emotional basis of their relationships and establish a deeper sense of intimacy and connection with their partners by engaging in shared experiences and rituals, embracing vulnerability and authenticity, developing empathy and compassion, and practising open and honest communication.

They can also cultivate mindfulness and presence.

Embracing these practices as novices in the field of erotic wizardry can result in significant revelations, healing, and transformation, enabling practitioners to move confidently, honourably, and reverently through the complex terrain of love and desire.

Exploring the intersection of emotional and sexual intimacy

The foundation of happy and meaningful relationships is the meeting point of emotional and sexual intimacy, providing erotic wizards with a fundamental path to increased fulfilment, trust, and connection with their partners. Sexual intimacy entails the physical expression of desire, pleasure, and passion, whereas emotional intimacy focuses on the sharing of ideas, feelings, and vulnerabilities. We explore the relationship between emotional and sexual intimacy in this section, looking at the ways in which these two domains interact and support one another.

We also provide practitioners with useful information and advice on navigating the complex terrain of love, desire, and connection. Sexual intimacy is predicated on emotional intimacy, which offers a solid base of vulnerability, trust, and understanding for physical intimacy to flourish. By disclosing one's deepest feelings, wishes, and thoughts to a reliable companion, emotional intimacy fosters a sense of closeness and connection that transcends the material world. By communicating honestly and openly, paying attention to their partner's worries and experiences, and showing empathy and understanding for their needs and wishes, practitioners of erotic wizardry can foster emotional connection. In order to enable a deeper and more satisfying experience of sexual intimacy with their partners, practitioners can provide a secure and supportive environment for exploration and expression by cultivating emotional closeness. On the other hand, sexual intimacy can also strengthen the emotional bond and closeness between couples by giving them a natural and physical outlet to express their thoughts, desires, and vulnerabilities. Sharing pleasure, passion, and vulnerability with a partner during sexual intimacy forges a unique and strong link that goes beyond words and deeds. Erotic wizardry practitioners can develop sexual intimacy by talking openly with their partners about their needs and boundaries, exploring their desires and fantasies, and partaking in pleasurable and connecting activities like sensual massage, tantric practices, or erotic storytelling. Through the acceptance of sexual intimacy, practitioners can strengthen their emotional bond with their partners and cultivate a sense of fulfilment, passion, and trust in their relationship. In addition, the quest for fulfilment and connection with a partner necessitates the integration of mind, body, and spirit at the intersection of emotional and sexual intimacy. By enabling a profound and meaningful connection, emotional intimacy promotes acceptance, understanding, and trust between couples. In contrast, sexual intimacy strengthens the physical and tactile bond of closeness between couples by enabling practitioners to express their wishes, passions, and vulnerabilities. Practitioners can develop a comprehensive and integrated approach to love, desire, and connection by investigating the junction of emotional and sexual intimacy. This will enable them to feel more fulfilled and satisfied in their relationships. For practitioners of erotic wizardry, investigating the intersection of emotional and sexual connection can also result in great understanding, healing, and transformation.

Through exploring their deepest wants, anxieties, and weaknesses with their partners, therapists can reveal previously unnoticed facets of their own identities and relationships, ultimately promoting personal development, healing, and connection. Practitioners can traverse the intricacies of love, desire, and connection with confidence, integrity, and reverence via open and honest conversation, vulnerability, and trust. This enables a more meaningful and fulfilling experience of intimacy and connection with their partners. In conclusion, practitioners of erotic wizardry have a transforming avenue to deeper connection, trust, and fulfilment in their relationships when they investigate the junction of emotional and sexual intimacy. Practitioners can build a solid foundation of trust and understanding with their partners by fostering emotional intimacy via vulnerability, open and honest communication, and empathy.

This paves the way for a more satisfying and profound experience of sexual intimacy. On the other hand, practitioners can enhance their emotional intimacy and connection by accepting sexual intimacy as a way to communicate their desire, passion, and vulnerability to their partners. This can lead to a feeling of fulfilment, trust, and passion in their relationship. As novices in the field of erotic wizardry, practitioners can navigate the complex terrain of love, desire, and connection with confidence, integrity, and reverence by embracing the junction of emotional and sexual intimacy, which can result in profound discoveries, healing and transformation.

Exercises for cultivating deeper connection with oneself and partners

In the world of erotic wizardry, great intimacy, pleasure, and contentment can only be attained by developing a closer bond with oneself and one's companions. Practitioners can go on a journey of self-discovery, inquiry, and transformation through a range of exercises and practices. They are able to create more fulfilling and meaningful relationships as a result, developing greater awareness of both themselves and their partners. This section offers insights and assistance for practitioners who want to increase their erotic experiences and uncover the transformational power of love and desire.

We explore numerous exercises for fostering deeper connections with oneself and partners. The discipline of self-reflection and introspection is a potent tool for developing a deeper connection with oneself and your partner. By devoting time to examining one's ideas, feelings, wants, and experiences, self-reflection enables practitioners to obtain a greater awareness of their needs, values, and objectives, as well as gain insight into their deepest selves. Through journaling, meditation, or other contemplative practices, people can become more self-aware and accepting, which will enhance their connection to themselves and lay the groundwork for more sincere and fulfilling relationships. Vulnerability and authenticity practice is another way to foster a deeper connection with partners and yourself. Being open and forthcoming with a trustworthy partner about one's worries, insecurities, and weaknesses is a necessary component of vulnerability. Conversely, authenticity is speaking the truth and being sincere while expressing one's feelings, ideas, and desires.

By accepting vulnerability and authenticity in their relationships and allowing themselves to be seen and appreciated for who they actually are, practitioners of erotic wizardry can create stronger connections with both themselves and their partners. This could entail being present and mindful of one another's wants and desires, as well as exchanging personal thoughts and feelings. Practitioners can establish a secure and encouraging environment for investigation and expression by encouraging openness and sincerity. This allows for the emergence of greater closeness and connection. Moreover, practising empathic communication and active listening is a way to foster a stronger connection with both partners and oneself. In order to listen actively, one must give their whole attention to what the other person is saying, without passing judgment or interjecting, and make an effort to comprehend their viewpoint and experiences. Empathic communication is acknowledging and respecting the experiences and sentiments of the other person while demonstrating empathy and understanding for their needs, thoughts, and feelings. By engaging in empathic communication and active listening in their relationships, practitioners of erotic wizardry can foster a stronger sense of connection with both themselves and their partners, making them feel heard, understood, and appreciated.

This might be putting electronics and other distractions away, focusing entirely on one another, and demonstrating compassion and understanding for one another's viewpoints and experiences.

Practitioners can increase their closeness and connection with themselves and their partners by practising active listening and empathetic communication. This strengthens the framework for love, trust, and understanding to grow. Additionally, sharing experiences and rituals with partners is a practice that fosters a stronger connection with oneself and others. Partners can improve their relationship, generate enduring memories, and deepen their bond via shared events and rituals. By participating in rituals and shared actions that are meaningful and personal to both partners, practitioners of erotic magic can foster deeper connections with both themselves and their partners. This could include going on romantic dates, taking trips together, commemorating milestones, or establishing customs and rituals that stand in for their dedication to one another.

Through exchanging experiences and customs, practitioners can establish a feeling of unity and belonging in their relationship, which strengthens the bond between them on an emotional level as well as their sense of partnership and companionship. In conclusion, erotic wizardry practitioners have a potent tool at their disposal for strengthening intimacy, trust, and fulfilment in their relationships: exercises for developing a deeper connection with oneself and their partners. Practitioners can lay a solid foundation for intimacy and connection to flourish by engaging in self-reflection and introspection, embracing vulnerability and authenticity, communicating empathically and actively listening, and sharing rituals and experiences with their partners. Accepting these exercises as novices in the field of erotic wizardry can result in deep realizations, healing, and transformation, enabling practitioners to move confidently, honourably, and reverently through the complex terrain of love, desire, and connection.

CONCLUSION

Within "The Beginner's Book of Erotic Wizardy: Mastering the Mystical Aspects of Love and Desire," readers travel through a voyage of sensuality, self-discovery, and exploration. This book provides practitioners with the tools and insights they need to cultivate greater pleasure, intimacy, and fulfillment, unlock the transformative power of love and desire, and deepen their connection with themselves and their partners through the exploration of mystical practices, sacred rituals, and intimate techniques.

Readers are encouraged to embrace the eroticism's mystical elements in order to access the rich tapestry of feelings, sensations, and energies that underlie their experiences of love and desire. This will enable them to manage the intricacies of personal relationships with dignity, confidence, and integrity.

Readers will find useful advice, inspiration, and wisdom to support them on their journey of erotic exploration and discovery, whether they are diving into the depths of their desires and fantasies, examining the intersection of emotional and sexual intimacy, or mastering the power of sensory stimulation.

"The Beginner's Book of Erotic Wizardy" is an invaluable tool for anybody looking to master the mystical aspects of love and desire and unleash the transformative potential of their intimate relationships because of its unique blend of spiritual wisdom, mystical insights, and practical counsel.

Thank you for buying and reading/ listening to our book. If you found this book useful/ helpful please take a few minutes and leave a review on the platform where you purchased our book. Your feedback matters greatly to us.